CU01003234

Excellence Through Pa

THE BUSINESS COACHING REVOLUTION

About the Author

Seán Weafer is managing director of The Prosper Group Ltd., a leading executive coaching practice comprised of coaches with backgrounds in sales, human resources and senior management development.

He personally works with senior business leaders, directors, entrepreneurs and in the ongoing development of the management and sales function within business.

Seán is a master coach trainer, training hundreds of business managers as internal management coaches and advises organisations on how to create "consultative" management cultures through the use of coaching. He is a magnetic conference speaker, speaking at conferences and meetings internationally, where he spreads the message (and the methods) of personal excellence in business and sales.

Seán would welcome comments and questions on his work and may be contacted by email at sean@seanweafer.com

THE BUSINESS COACHING REVOLUTION

SEÁN WEAFER

Foreword by
Dr Denis Waitley

BLACKHALL
Publishing

This book was typeset by Gough Typesetting Services for
Blackhall Publishing,
8 Priory Hall, Stillorgan,
Co. Dublin,
Ireland.
and
Blackhall Publishing,
2025 Hyperion Avenue,
Los Angeles,
CA 90027,
USA.

Email: blackhall@eircom.net
Website: www.blackhallpublishing.com

A catalogue record for this book is available from the British
Library

ISBN: PB: 1 842180 24 X
HB: 1 842180 30 4

Printed in Ireland by
ColourBooks Ltd

Dedication

For my darling Sharon and for Nicholas.
For my mother Eileen and for my dad Peter.
Lastly, for Mam and Dad Hurley.

Contents

Preface

My attention was captured recently by a press report of a UK study stating that training improved effectiveness by 28 per cent, whereas training plus coaching improved effectiveness by up to 88 per cent. The figures are quite startling when one considers the amount of corporate finance invested in training personnel and the, as yet, relatively small amount committed to ensuring suitable business coaching programmes are in place to support that training.

Partly this is because of the limited understanding of the systems, effects and benefits that come from business coaching. This book is written to provide some further understanding of, specifically, business coaching and some of the thinking behind a successful firm that specialises in the fields of management and sales coaching.

Executive or business coaching has grown in prominence since the late 1990s and has become an increasingly popular and established intervention for the challenges that face company leadership. This is particularly evident to me in the increasing numbers of "hard-nosed" business executives who are happy to confirm that they use the services of an executive coach.

Excellence Through Partnership: The Business Coaching Revolution is also written to provide some professional guidelines to prospective business coaches and a "what to watch for" if one is a management, HR or training professional charged with "buying-in" the service.

Coaching is evolving as a profession in its own right,

but it is still early days and at present it is useful to have some guidelines of this sort.

I have from time to time been asked what attracted me to coaching, what it is that excites me about this new profession. The answer is that I enjoy the opportunity of helping people evolve to higher levels of personal and professional development. The ability to interface with people and thus draw out more of their natural (and often hidden) abilities, allowing them greater freedom of choice in how they conduct their business ventures and balance their lives is what intrigues and excites me the most.

I have always been fascinated by what the magic is within people and coaching is a pathway for releasing that magic for performance and profit, for both my clients and those whose lives they touch.

I hope that you enjoy and profit from reading this book and look forward to hearing from you with your feedback and experiences.

Seán Weafer
Dublin,
June, 2001.

Foreword

Because you are reading this foreword, I am assuming that you bought this book, were given it as a gift, have borrowed it or are browsing through it to see if you want to add it to your library. By reading it and internalising the principles herein, you will be gaining "The Edge" over your competitors.

There is a fine line, a winner's edge, separating the top 5 per cent in the champion's circle – the real achievers – from the rest of society. On the PGA tour, only a few strokes per year separate the top money earners from the rest of the touring professionals. In the World Cup and Olympic Games the only difference between the trophy and gold-medal winners and the non-medal winners is a fraction of time, distance or points.

So it is in business and in your personal life, where the playing field is anything but level. The consistent, enduring leaders in professional and personal arenas have special knowledge, attitudes, skills and habits in common that make them so uncommonly successful. Their advantage is not based upon talent, IQ or luck but rather on decisions and actions that have become an integral part of their daily lives.

This book is designed to transform managers into leaders, so they can coach employees into becoming entrepreneurs in a global marketplace where everyone is at risk and employment is not guaranteed. In order to get ahead today, individuals must reinvent themselves as companies and institutions restructure the way they function.

In the past, change in business and social life was incremental, and a set of personal strategies for achieving excellence was not required. Today, in the knowledge-based world where the shelf life of your formal education is no more than eighteen months and where change is the rule, a set of personal strategies is essential to success, even survival. Never again will you be able to go to your place of business on autopilot, comfortable and secure that the organisation will provide for and look after you.

In order to lead others, we must first lead ourselves. In order to gain the confidence and respect of others, we must first set a positive example. You and I must look in the mirror when we ask who is responsible for our success or failure.

In a world in which working with other people is essential, lifelong learning means deepening your understanding of yourself and others. A shared belief emerged from a recent round-table discussion among a group of innovative multi-national business leaders. All the leaders, while innovating in their business lives, were doing the same in other spheres of their lives. They agreed that their subordinates' executive growth depended on personal growth and that those who believed they had completed their education were on a fast track to personal obsolescence. Lifelong learning, once a luxury for the few, has become absolutely vital to continued success.

In my work with Apollo astronauts and Olympic athletes, I have discovered the critical role that coaches and mentors play in their achievements. The true mission of a great coach is to help uncover and develop the potential of the individual toward peak performance.

Seán Weafer has become an outstanding coach and mentor. He has the ability to assimilate complex concepts in effective human behaviour and convert them into interesting and informative lessons in leadership. Oceans apart in our environmental and cultural upbringing, Seán and I have experienced synergy together in an unspoken professional partnership and peer relationship in helping leaders lead.

His book *Excellence Through Partnership: The Business Coaching Revolution* is on target and laser accurate. There never was a winner who didn't have a winning coach.

As you read and grasp the underlying significance of the principles in the pages that follow, you will understand – as I have – that we are accelerating in fast forward into a world where experts, who defend what they have learned, are dinosaurs; and where coaches and those who are "coach able" will rule the future.

Dr Denis Waitley
Author of *The Psychology of Winning*

Acknowledgements

This book would not have been written without the help and encouragement of several people.

First, my friend and business partner Jonathan Bell, from whom I have learned so much in our time together. Secondly, Dr Denis Waitley, who has been both friend and mentor to Jonathan and myself for several years now.

I would also like to thank my publishers Blackhall Publishing for their initial approach to write the book and for keeping me to deadlines, the essence of coaching.

All my coaching colleagues and trainers in the Prosper Group and First Coach International who share their knowledge, their good humour and company in our work together.

My wife Sharon and son Nicholas, for their patience in putting up with an absent husband and daddy during what is a time-consuming process.

Lastly, my clients with whom I have the pleasure of sharing unique experiences, conquests, accomplishments and their ascension to new thresholds of performance. Without them I would not have the opportunity to pursue my passion of helping others self-actualise.

THE PROSPER GROUP LTD.

The Prosper Group Ltd. was founded by Seán Weafer and Jonathan Bell in 1994. The company is an executive coaching practice which specialises in coaching industry leaders, entrepreneurs and sales professionals.

The company also specialises in facilitating management teams, improving inter-team dynamics and high-level sales and management communications skills training. In addition, the company trains managers and individuals in professional coaching and mentoring skills.

The company is based in Dublin, Ireland. They may be contacted by email at info@prosper-group.com. The company website is worth visiting at www.prosper-group.com. The company produces a regular magazine, which can be subscribed to on request.

CHAPTER ONE

The Coaching Paradigm

"We are beings caught between peaks of unlimited consciousness and valleys of self-limiting imaginings."

WHY BUSINESS COACHING?

Imagine a business world where people are happy in their positions, effective in their work and self-directed in their efforts. Imagine senior business executives effortlessly managing stressful environments, making effective decisions, taking action without hesitation, communicating clearly, living more balanced lives and maximising their personal potential for achievement on a consistent basis.

Now imagine a business world that uses the benefits of the high-tech revolution and marries it seamlessly to the people skills of the high-touch revolution. A new revolution is breaking upon corporate shores – a revolution in maximising the human capital of our people, and it is being led by business coaching.

Business coaching is about effective and efficient individual, team and organisational performance. It is a change in business management culture effected at an individual level that profoundly impacts on the organisation as a whole. It does this through achieving consistent, specific and measurable results from people in a consultative, non-directive way; a way that gathers the very best of the coach and the individual being coached and forges it into something more than either would have accomplished alone. It is how management can come to delegate more effectively, through switching on the desire of their staff to initiate change willingly. It enables individual business executives to realise their potential to achieve higher levels of personal and business performance. It raises levels of individual commitment to personal and corporate success and it helps unleash the true potential of the person being coached. Business coaching engages people in a systematic process and a discipline focused on personal excellence and business success. The ultimate goal of this process is the personal fulfilment and empowerment of the individual being coached – and the consistent achievement of corporate goals as the result of this.

Business (or executive) coaching is about harmonising the goals of the individual and the organisation. Just how it does that and why it is evolving into a modern business phenomenon and into a new business profession is the subject of this book. Coaching is increasingly accepted as a skill all managers should have and should practice with staff but, to date, the emphasis has been on coaching as some form of problem-solving intervention designed to effect remedial action. Often coaching has been viewed as a "competency" of management rather than as a style of management itself.

However, the practice of coaching within an organisation needs to be viewed quite differently. It needs to be viewed not as a management intervention or as a "competency" but as a specific practice and process of day-to-day management of organisations and teams. It *is* management for the new century. I would also propose that coaching is not just a skill of internal managers; it is a business service for all professionals and owner/managers that should be provided by suitably qualified and registered external executive coaching practitioners, not unlike the business services provided currently by accountants, lawyers or management consultants.

Effective coaching practice, therefore, is nothing short of a radical re-consideration of the services of management to the practice of successful business for the information age. This view is at variance with traditional management practice in that it takes into consideration a critical element of business success – the *personal meaning* attached to the actions that create this success by the person undertaking the action.

We have all at one time paused to admire the challenges that successful people in business faced and overcame in their pursuit of business excellence and success. The general assumption tends to be that they have been exceptional in some way, or just lucky, by being in the right place at the right time. Yet luck is often defined as "when preparation meets opportunity". The defining characteristic of an enterprises' "overnight success" often seems to be that it takes years of personal preparation and experience on the part of its principals to recognise and grasp the opportunity when it presents itself. If so, then something else is at work that allows such successful people to forge their way to the top in business. I suggest that the critical factor omitted from managing personnel in the workplace, which empowers the results that successful business coaches/managers get from their team members/ clients, is personal meaning – the prime value that we attach to the decisions we make and the actions we subsequently take.

The models I use to design our coach trainings and coaching service are threefold. The first model is based on the inherent need for a client to self-actualise or to be the best that they can be and to see meaning in that purpose.

The second model concerns the ability to change the client's perspective on, or perception of, the context in which they may find themselves when they first come for coaching. By being able to change a client's perception of their context, we can help them to generate new solutions to old challenges, much like one's levels of stress changes as one changes one's attitude to the stressor. The third model is that of excellence in communication – both with oneself and with others: with oneself, to gain a greater sense of self-awareness and motivation; and with others, to gain the ability to communicate clearly one's needs and to harmonise them with the needs of others for maximum performance.

The first model is based on the work of Abraham Maslow, whose theory of the Hierarchy of Needs proposes that the desire for humans to self-actualise is the highest of all needs. This, I believe, is the essence of mankind's search for meaning and it is what drives us to higher and higher levels of evolution. It could be considered as a driver towards excellence that is "hard-wired" into our psychological and behavioural systems. The second model draws from the work of Carl Jung, whose work in the fields of human preferences and perception is used in many areas. The third and final model is based on the skills of Neuro Linguistic Programming (NLP), a field that focuses on, among other things, the development of effective communications processes and skills.

The area of NLP is recognised as a rich field of techniques and models that assist us to evolve our thinking to higher levels, to gain a greater sense of self-understanding, to gain greater control over our personal states (or emotions, which drive our decisions and hence our actions) and provide the tools necessary to communicate the realisations of that self-understanding to the people around us. At this point, we might pause to consider what NLP stands for:

N stands for Neuro or the neural system (including the brain, spinal cord and radial nerves) – the many live nerve connections of which our human system is composed. So dense is this number of live nerve connections that it is "guestimated" by neurobiologists at somewhere in the region of 10 to the power of 10 to the power of 10. This number is supposedly greater than the number of every grain of sand on every beach and desert in the world today – and all of this in the body of just one human being. To quote Hamlet "What a piece of work is Man".

L stands for Linguistics, which has to do with language – how we use it, the pictures it paints in our minds and how our behaviours are effected by these pictures – holistic pictures that create behavioural responses. Sit in your favourite restaurant, chose your favourite dish from the menu and notice your response: you "see" and "smell" the dish, and your mouth begins to water – yet it's only words on a page, not the food itself, that is in front of us. The words have caused the response.

P stands for Programming. This relates to the "strategies" that people use in everything they do – from making decisions about how they eat their food to decisions about life and business. When you eat your dinner do you leave your favourite item on the plate until last or do you take a little bit of it to compliment the food on the plate that you like least? Know anyone who will not eat their morning toast unless it's buttered right out to the edges?

Everyone uses strategies that are unique to them. Through coaching we sometimes need to challenge and reframe those strategies if they are not supportive of the desired performance of the client.

Personal coaching today is evolving into many forms. Recognising partnership as a basis for individual excellence is increasingly accepted in Western society. Perhaps the most usual form of coaching that we are familiar with is the relationship between the sports coach and the athlete. This relationship is based on a mutual trust and an exchange of information for the benefit of the athlete's performance. With the help of a sports coach, the athlete learns to maximise their physical and mental potential to a higher degree than that which they might otherwise have reached on their own.

We have only to look at the top athletes in the arena of sports today from golf to basketball to see the effect an inspiring, challenging and knowledgeable coach can have on the performance of an athlete. In the past, the coach remained a shadowy figure, recognised only by the athlete and the close circle of people that surrounded them. An almost Svengali-like figure who ruled the life of the athlete with a rod of iron. They were often products of a similar school themselves, serving as coaches because of their own past successes in the field of play.

Today sports coaches enjoy a more public profile as the increasing public popularity and media interest in sports has raised the profile of the coaches as well as the athletes – a rising tide raising all boats. Names such as Leadbetter in golf highlight the profile of these once "backroom boys" whose effects on the game are enormous and who can command high fees for the benefit of their expertise.

But modern coaches are a different breed. Like the coaches of old they too have set about learning as much as they can about their chosen sport. They have learned the theory and practice of excellence. They have learned what it takes to create winners. Unlike the coaches of old, however, it is increasingly unlikely that they have ever played the game in which they coach today's winners.

Today the emphasis of coaching is still placed on the physical and the technical aspect of the game but also increasingly on a more vital factor – the mental strategies that create the winning edge that sets the superstars of sport apart from the mainstream. In fact, today it is not unusual to find coaches who specialise in the "mind game" more than the physical game. A critical element of that mental edge is the energy that the athlete empowers their actions with, energy drawn from the meaning or value they place on their success.

Business coaching is based on this same principle – that of honing the mind-set of business coaching clients so that they can marshal their mental and physical resources to achieve more than they would working alone. It plays an increasingly important part in delivering measurable and tangible results to executives and business people who face greater and greater challenges in maximising their potential, within ever more limiting time frames. To meet these challenges, business people are turning to a new breed of professional business coach whose job is to ensure a "yes" answer to the following question:

> *At this moment, are you doing everything you know you are capable of doing to effect the greatest amount of change in your life/career and reaping the satisfaction that should be coming with that accomplishment?*

It is worth reading that again. In that one question is the essence of the challenge that faces us all: focusing on the most important thing we should be doing all the time; being all that we can be.

For most of us the answer to the question is "no". The excuse we usually give is "lack of time" and that "if I could only manage my time more effectively I could be doing this". Unfortunately, it is not just about time. Time management is a fallacy – we cannot manage what we do not control. Is it possible to make an hour longer than it is, bring yesterday back into today or recoup those lost years and invest them in future opportunities? No.

The answer then lies elsewhere, with something that we *do* control – our focus. Once we control our focus and our intent time exists to serve us. Two things more are necessary: discipline and an external view for effective feedback and corrective action. All these things come from effective coaching.

However, it often seems that a clear definition of business coaching or executive coaching today is lacking. Therefore, let me offer a specific definition of coaching and then clarify how it differs from both mentoring and therapy of any kind. Business coaching may be defined as:

> *A collaborative partnership between a business coach/manager and their client/team member and a system which identifies perceived obstacles, generates new solutions, sets objectives and implements agreed actions based on holding the client/team member accountable to themselves.*

It is worth exploring this definition further. By *collaborative* I mean that coaching is something that relies on the synergy of two people to accomplish more than either would alone. In effect, that coaching is the achievement of excellence through partnership. It is a *system* because it utilises a structure and sequence that leads to the definition and solution of *perceived* obstacles. By *perceived* I mean that often a client or staff member may be finding some difficulty in handling certain challenges, because they are too caught up in the immediate perspective of the challenge. By being able to change their perspective or their way of looking at the challenge, a coach can assist the client to find new solutions or new ways of overcoming such challenges. I sometimes call this the "crossword syndrome". Have you ever attempted a crossword and found yourself stuck on one word – just one word that would open up the solution to the crossword? No matter how hard you try you cannot find that word and then someone leans over your shoulder, reads the clue and says "that's such and such" and suddenly, seemingly without effort, they have resolved the problem? That's because that person was able to take a "meta view" of the problem. This view is above the immediate perspective of the problem, as it does not emotionally impact on the person's success or failure. As such they were perfectly able to find the solution. Coaches, not personally dependent on the consequences of the challenge, often provide such "solution suggestions" to their clients.

Solution, Objective and *Action*, the process by which a coach breaks the global challenge into the "bite size" pieces from which all great endeavours can be accomplished. It is said that extraordinary businesses are not accomplished by extraordinary people; they are accomplished by ordinary people who do ordinary things extraordinarily well. Simple actions mean guaranteed results.

Lastly, *Accountability* is the key to coaching success: the willingness of clients/staff to be held accountable to themselves (not the coach) for delivering on the actions, which they play a part in defining. Without the disciplined input of the coach and the willingness of the client to accept personal accountability the process would fail.

So given this definition, how does coaching differ from mentoring and therapy? First, coaching differs from mentoring in that coaching is *non-industry specific*. In other words it is independent of the work that the person being coached (the "coachee", as opposed to the "client" or organisation they work for) is doing. Coaches focus on the development and empowerment of the individual. As part of the process, they consider the additional resources or training that a person may need to be successful, although the coach does not necessarily provide such training. The coach focuses on the development of the *person* not the *role*. As such, someone trained in coaching can be brought in to effect change anywhere. They effect change in the role by developing the individual and their performance, not the role itself. In most cases, a coach may have little or no knowledge of the specifics of the work carried out by the coachee unless it is "objective relevant". It is the coachee who will bring change to the role. It is the empowerment of the coachee that returns power to the individual to actively engage in effecting positive and productive change.

In mentoring, while the same techniques can be used, the emphasis is different. Here the emphasis is very much on the passing on of a specific skill-set for a particular role. Here the mentor may provide highly specific skills education and will primarily focus on the development of the *skills* needed for the role and not necessarily the person.

The difference between coaching and therapy is more distinct. In a very simplified definition (with apologies to professional therapists) it would be that therapy is a process focused on resolving past events that effect current behaviours. The emphasis is on emotional or psychological issues that, once resolved, can improve the present behaviour of the person. Therapy, of necessity, looks into the past and the conditioning that created the present. Coaching, however, is a process that focuses on improving future history by the full use of the client's current and potential resources. It focuses on the future and the present decisions that will create it.

Coaching has become very much a "buzz" word over the last few years, but I believe that it is more than a passing trend in management practice. I believe that coaching is fundamentally evolving, not just as a replacement for current management practice, but also as a profession in its own right. As the knowledge and practice of coaching grows, it is highly likely that for business people in the future a business coach will be as important a member of their professional advisory team as a lawyer or an accountant.

So who is using coaching today? As we will see in a later chapter, everyone – from business owners, chief executives and senior directors to middle managers, team leaders and sales people – is benefiting from using professional external coaches today. For each one the need for the coach is different.

Often for business owners and chief executives, coaching serves as a partnership to help them focus their thinking on the organisation and acts as a sounding board for their ideas, even generating new ideas and helping them focus on more effective planning and communication strategies for their organisations. It helps overcome a lot of the isolation felt by such executives and holds them accountable for continued innovation within the company.

For senior directors and managers, apart from the challenge of working "on" rather than "in" their departments, there are often issues of positioning and profile within companies that they need to address, securing what has been achieved by more innovative and high profile projects generated through interaction with a coach.

Team leaders, often plucked from the floor and given responsibility without prior preparation (particularly in dot.com cultures), may need support in the development of a coaching culture within their teams that assists in the learning of positive processes by which they can lead and empower in a consultative manner people who may have until recently been their peers.

For sales people the emphasis is often on personal focus and confidence, raising the standards for them, leading them to accomplishments beyond those they would have achieved alone, encouraging them to develop and apply their personal abilities to accomplish measurable and quantifiable increases in their sales.

In all cases, coaching brings the synergy and the accountability to effect change. What effects change at a personal level, the leverage, is uniquely different in each case and we train clients to identify, access and use that leverage to effect the desired change. In effect, coaches act as catalysts of change – first helping a client to identify their desired outcomes and then providing whatever is necessary to effect the action that brings change. After the action is initiated they engage in a process of alternating, reinforcing and balancing feedback to keep their client/ staff member on track to reach the goals that have been mutually defined.

The demand for properly trained professional external coaches is increasing all the time, in tandem with the increase in hours being put into careers and workplaces. The need to have an external or objective overview, free of the limiting thoughts and views that, of necessity, often define a person's role within an organisation, is powerful and creates rapid and lasting change in productivity and job satisfaction.

Of course there are internal coaches too, managers who understand the importance of the consultative approach and who accomplish for their teams and organisations results that their more traditional colleagues fail to realise. Internal coaches engage in an active process of renewing a company's daily or weekly focus, ensuring that the people who deliver on the goals of the organisation are constantly motivated by the harmonising of staff's personal goals with the overall goals of the team and/or organisation.

A problem with the perception of internal company coaching up to this point has been the belief that coaching is primarily something applied to those who are failing to perform. When positioning coaching we always ask that it is viewed and developed as a means of "fast-tracking" the best people and applied accordingly. Often this improves the perception of the process in the eyes of its recipient when such coaching is undertaken in an in-company context.

For external coaches, however, this positive expectation of the results of coaching is often easier to achieve, as the fact that they are external to the organisation indicates an investment in a proven process geared towards success. In many cases, it will always be that senior company figures may only be coached by external coaches due to interpersonal issues, appropriateness of seniority and the critical and confidential nature of their roles.

Within an organisation there are two objectives to coaching: one is to enhance performance; the other is to identify remedial action and bring it into effect prior to a problem occurring with a staff member. In *performance coaching* the goal is simple: assist the individual to maximise their personal performance and thus the impact they have within the organisation. Here we often already have a successful client but we are engaging with them to help them pass through a higher performance threshold. The reasons why they would wish to do this will have already been elicited and implemented within the process. In *remedial coaching* the goal is to anticipate a problem or resolve one that is already occurring. Again, the positive and willing engagement of the coachee is an important part of the process and they are encouraged to find and implement solutions to the problem, rather than having blame apportioned to them. The emphasis is on the learning and the consequences of the application of that learning.

There is also a great deal of talk about "life" coaching and "business" coaching. The boundaries between the two have been a little blurred, mainly because of the slow acceptance of the importance of the individual's feelings and values when it comes to business. As there is little valid certification or professional qualifications in this emerging field, pretty much anyone can set up shop as a "coach". While this will change with time, as professional institutes evolve, the best way to determine the coach ideal for your needs is to look at the company offering the service: is it a practice or is it an individual? What is its existing client-base? Does it have a professional code of ethics? Does it have professional indemnity insurance? Do its members have relevant experience, standardised training processes and are they clear on the goals of their own practice?

These are just some of the ways one might identify a suitable provider of executive or business coaching. We will look at this further in Chapter 7 – Introducing Coaching into Organisations.

CHAPTER TWO

A Brief History of Coaching

Business coaching, or executive coaching as it is also known, is one answer to the increasing problem of less time/more demands within all forms of business venture, whether they are team-driven corporations or owner-managed small enterprises.

But there are other problems manifesting themselves within the work environment that coaching can address: problems such as the greater utilisation of human capital and the coming to terms with changed social dynamics and values of the workplace that conditions the behaviour of such capital.

These social dynamics have resulted in less respect for authority for authority's sake, less willingness to accept directive rather than co-operative management structures, less staff loyalty to the company leading to greater mobility in the workforce and a greater appreciation by the staff of their individual identity. This increasingly manifests itself in a desire for more flexible working hours, greater recognition for personal contribution and respect of personal values.

Why are these issues presenting themselves at this time? To find the answer we need to look briefly at the greater social picture and the effects of better education, media generation of higher expectations and the increasing search for greater meaning and value in people's lives.

In the mid-20th century the numbers moving from primary to secondary and then on to tertiary education were comparatively few compared to the numbers that enjoy such opportunities now. The foundation of widespread and generally free education in the West over the last few decades has provided higher standards of education to a larger group of people than ever before in the history of society. It has provided the education that has fuelled the present information age and the move from an industrial-based society to a society where one of the most important forms of business capital is that of information and knowledge.

Education is an important factor in the conditioning that creates our values and hence our beliefs. Conditioning itself is created from many sources: apart from education, our social situation, family structure, spiritual beliefs, peers and so on are all contributing factors. All of the above have undergone significant change in the last few decades. In addition, the "pillars of society" (church, state, big business and so on) in which people traditionally placed a great deal of trust have been found lacking too often for that faith to remain.

This loss of faith in centuries-old models of behaviour has caused an increase in the number of people seeking their own answers, finding their own path to meaning in their life and work. It has also resulted in a more challenging attitude towards authority. In the past, people would seldom question the word of a teacher, policeman, politician, professional – such as a lawyer, barrister, accountant, or even their own "place" in society. Now that has changed. The impact of this social change is being felt in the workplace where the role of the manager is, of necessity, in a process of change.

Now the emphasis in management training is increasingly on people development, communications skills and relationship management. Skills that are termed the "soft skills" of management were often overlooked in the traditional style of management, which tended towards an authoritative and paternalistic approach.

Improved education and changed conditions have also raised our expectations above mere survival. Over the last several generations, despite war and economic recession – or perhaps because of it, each generation has improved substantially above the one prior to it. The lives of our grandparents were significantly different from ours today. Ours has become a materially richer society, but one where consumerism and acquisition have arguably replaced the more human and community-based values of earlier generations. The media has served to fuel such material expectations and the bombardment of our homes each evening through television, radio, magazine, news print and now the Internet has continued the rise in personal expectations. But the rise in our expectations as a result of our improved education and enhanced material expectations has also changed the nature of the relationships that we maintain within the workplace.

In the past, the position of a manager was almost sacred. Management was of a style that directed an employee to perform and expected such performance without question. A manager's word was law and they decided the fate of those who worked below them. Organisations were created on an almost institutional basis. They were large, almost military-like structures whose hierarchal framework ensured that power travelled from the top down. Such organisations mirrored the type of society people lived in.

Only gradually, with the growth in the power of trade unionism, were the individual's needs considered. But management continued to direct. Morale was never an issue: the phrase "firings will continue until morale improves" aptly sums up the attitude of the time.

Loyalty to a firm was unconditionally expected. Many

employees were employed from cradle to grave – held there not just by the politics of the workplace but by the expectations of a society that valued permanency and security of tenure. At one time, the greatest hold that authoritative management had over people was the fear of losing one's job. The consequences of this, including the shame, personal devaluation and loss of social status often associated with unemployment, were powerful motivators for compliance without question.

But by the late 20th century economic crises and recessions, and the willingness of firms to shed people *en masse*, regardless of loyalty or years of service, resulted in a difficult awakening to the new environment of downsizing and redundancy. This awakening created a new kind of culture in the workplace, a culture in which the individual reluctantly began to accept that loyalty counted for little and that they needed to look to themselves to survive the changing times ahead. A new philosophy was starting to emerge from the past, where the employee was dependant on the company for their future and security, to the present, where the employee recognises their intellectual capital is that which gives the company its strength.

Company management was learning to recognise that the success of the company was reliant on the degree of interdependence of the many skilled individuals who work together. The age of flat line management and self-directed teams was nascent.

But these teams were no longer composed of the traditional employee profile. Something else happened in the time of recession and another new culture was born – a culture of personal enterprise and acceptance of change as an axiom of the modern workplace. The day of the contractor, the self-employed consultant, the tele-worker and the mobile employee had arrived. Increasing numbers of a new kind of employee began to enter the workplace from the downsized organisations of the past. Contractors, consultants, work outplacement specialists, who worked by the hour and who owed loyalty only to their pay cheque and themselves, began to take their place in the modern organisation, working alongside those who still held the old traditional sense of employee. A new ethos began to enter the workplace – that of personal empowerment. The employee began to see themselves as valuable in their own right – as their own boss, independent of the workplace. The employee was becoming an entrepreneur.

The concept of self-directed and flat-line managed teams was designed to bring a greater cost-effectiveness and faster management communications to companies; a better means of effecting change at a more immediate level to respond to the rapid changes in the new marketplace. In a sense it was also designed to empower the employee, as they were to be recognised as an integral part of the team. "Team building" became the new phrase. But in the rush to embrace team building, company leaders had neglected a number of important components in making their teams work.

The first was the effect that the new form of team structure, which did away with the many layers of hierarchal privilege that had previously existed, would have on existing managers. This structure placed senior management for the first time in face-to-face, frontline, operational roles. The effect was enormous on veteran managers used to direction and obedience, suddenly working closer than ever with employees whose expectations had changed, who now viewed themselves as inherently valuable, whose sense of loyalty was no longer to the company but to themselves and who were becoming increasingly more mobile in the marketplace. Their training was inadequate to handle the changes in work practice and their proximity to people with whom they may never have had to converse in the past. Their skills were outdated and they still saw directive management continuing unchanged, unquestioned and unchecked at more senior levels.

The second was the speedy growth of technology and "dot.com" businesses. This growth led to more technicians and younger people being given management responsibility, which in the old economy would not have come their way for some time. With nothing to fall back on, a poor understanding of management and now expected to manage others who may have been their peers only yesterday, the new executives needed to find a new management system.

The third had been the dream of management for some time. This dream was that some day a way would be found to create self-empowered, self-motivated and self-directed teams that would ease the burden of managers who had come to be working more "IN" their teams – doing the work they were hiring others for, rather than "ON" their teams – leading by example and well thought out strategies.

The fourth was the lack of a process and a discipline that would guarantee results, while allowing everyone, both management and team members, full participation and the opportunity to benefit personally, to be fulfilled in their work and, therefore, motivated by the challenges they faced as a team and as an organisation.

The time had come for a new and radical approach to management. The answer was employee-centred management facilitation through a new style of manager – the team coach. Senior management would still set the objectives. These objectives would then be communicated through the organisation by coaching team members to an appreciation of the importance of their personal contribution and the personal benefit to be gained in the process of achieving corporate plans.

The age of the corporate coach has arrived.

CHAPTER THREE

Models of Coaching

Our organisation has evolved some distinct models by which we define what is occurring within coaching and coaching's place in the modern learning organisation. These are the Alpha-Beta Model and the Performance Loop, both of which indicate the factors driving the individual, and the CLIP model, which defines coaching's (or mentoring's) place within the modern organisation.

THE ALPHA-BETA MODEL

For many people without coaching, their performance consists of "peaks and troughs": highs of performance followed by lows of inactivity, lost focus, lost motivation and poor productivity. Often we have this kind of performance because we are attempting to be motivated "away" from something we fear, rather than "towards" something we desire. Figure 3.1 depicts this situation diagrammatically.

According to Sigmund Freud, humans are motivated away from pain and towards pleasure, and there is much value in this concept. In our work we maintain that everyone has a personal agenda that defines their performance and that often, as coaches, we have to help people identify what that is, help them define it and then give them permission to pursue it.

In a basic sense we all have values – abstract and global concepts such as freedom, happiness, love and so forth that we are pursuing. These values are powerful in that

Figure 3.1: Boom & Bust Syndrome

**Get motivated,
set goals,
start
improving
performance**

**Then motivation
fades, you hit a
challenge, have
a bad day and
performance
drops to old levels**

they define our motivation. However, whether we are living and working in accordance or in conflict with our values determines how successfully motivated we can be.

For most of us, we are moving away from what is contrary to our values – poverty, dependency, unemployment – so we are driven and motivated by the desire to avoid such things. When such things present a real danger to us we work hard to create an environment where we are free of them. As long as this motivates us we perform successfully. But as soon as we find ourselves no longer threatened by them, we slow down our pace, start to take it easy, lose our focus – the urgency has gone and with it our motivation to succeed. Then our performance starts to fade and fall off until such time as the things we wish to avoid present a threat again. We then speed up our pace, get focused and motivated, and performance improves – only to fall off again in the course of time.

So a cycle of motivation/de-motivation, productivity/

no productivity, performance/no performance exists for us. What is lost is consistency, consistency that leads to excellence. However, if we are working "towards" values that empower us – wealth, freedom, happiness, if we constantly re-set our sights so that we never settle for what we have settled for in the past, if we learn and are supported to raise our standards – coached to become all that we can be, then performance is different. We become people who create the world that others wake up to in the morning. This is the true power of the understanding of self-actualisation.

When we reach the goals we set ourselves, instead of our performance falling off, we just plateau for a short while, enjoy our victories, share the fruits of the journey with our coach and fellow traveller. Then we raise our sights again, towards new horizons, surpassing ourselves in the pursuit of excellence. Becoming all that we can be.

Let me ask you a question: at the present time are *you* accomplishing everything that you know *you* are capable of accomplishing and reaping the rewards that should go with that? If, like me, the answer is no, then welcome to 99 per cent of the human race. If, by any chance, the answer is yes, then wait – things will change. Change is life and life is change. We define this simple question with the Alpha-Beta model.

Figure 3.2: Alpha-Beta Model

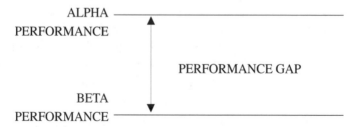

The Beta level is us, working as hard as we can, keeping up with the pace of the work and life style, applying all our energies. The Alpha level is all we know we can be, but seldom reach. The gap between the two is the *Performance Gap*, what separates us from our complete self – something that we seldom become on our own.

A coach works in the performance gap, helping the client find ways to improve their performance by 10, 20 or even 30 per cent over the existing Beta level. We do this by identifying the empowering values, tying them to specific objectives, breaking it down into actionable chunks and ensuring that the client has the power, the support and the accountability built in to the process to ensure they have the consistency of high performance. We call this "going from the global to the specific".

The interesting thing is that no matter how far we raise the Beta levels of clients, the Alpha level is impossible to reach: as the client realises the ability they actually possess, their belief in what they are capable of (the Alpha level) increases also. So we embark on the journey of helping businesses evolve to ever higher levels through the evolution of their leaders and their personnel.

THE PERFORMANCE LOOP

This model (Figure 3.3) is a means of explaining what defines performance within us – the factors that influence our ability to be all that we can be.

The first part of this process is *conditioning*. Conditioning affects everything else and in our formative years it is an entirely unconscious process of personal programming. There are three distinct stages of conditioning.

In stage one, the *imprinting* stage, which usually occurs

Figure 3.3: The Performance Loop

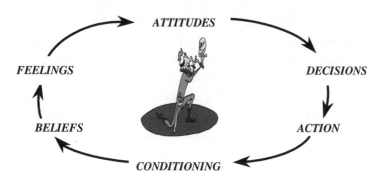

between zero and seven years of age, we learn the basic rules of survival. Our critical models at this time are our parents, our siblings and our peers. They affect our evolving self-concept (our core self-beliefs), which affects our emerging personalities. Our reading, listening and viewing material, significant authority figures (or lack of same) – such as teachers, clergy and police, also impact upon our impressionable minds. At this stage we have little critical faculties and often the experiences and learnings that we take on board at this time are taken on without suitable analysis or informed choice. In stage two, the *modelling* stage, we begin to select key figures that we model our behaviours on. These may be parents, in-laws or even mythological/superhuman heroes. In stage three, the *socialisation* stage, from 14 years to 21 years, we are evolving as individuals, sensing our independence, ironically through learning group (or gang) behaviour.

All of this conditioning leads to the development of our critical values, the abstract and global concepts we read about in the last model. From our values hang our *beliefs*, which we hold to be true about ourselves and about the world around us. Henry Ford, the founder of the Ford Motor Company, said, "if you believe you can or if believe you can't – you're right", indicating that it is our beliefs that determine our futures. Everyone comes to coaching with a distinct set of beliefs. Some of these beliefs are empowering and support the individual, and some are beliefs that sabotage a person's ability to be all that they can be.

From beliefs emanate our emotions or *feelings*. Despite popular misconception, it is our feelings that determine our decisions. Much as we like to think that we are logical and clinical when making decisions – weighing up all the pros and cons of the situation, carefully analysing the facts, the truth is that all our decisions come down to whether the consequences of such decisions will bring us pain or pleasure. So, if we wish to influence people to make decisions that they might not have made without a coach's intercession, an important part of that intervention is showing the client where the benefit or pleasure is to be gained by trying something new or different.

From emotions or feelings come our *attitudes*: our interface with the world outside of ourselves; the face we present, or would like to present, to the world. Attitudes are conveyed to others by the level of congruity that we demonstrate when we communicate with others. Congruity, or congruence, is when what we feel is genuine and is reflected in the language of our body, voice tonality and spirit. In subtle ways we can empower or defeat the message we present to the world depending on whether we are emotionally committed to the outcome. Can we tell the difference between people who really are not interested and are pretending they are and someone who is passionately committed to something?

From attitudes we take our *decisions* – from which change develops. We can chose to make a decision, or make a decision not to make a decision. Either way the world changes for the better or worse. Making a decision, committing to something, is the single most important change that can occur within a human being. Making a decision to act marshals our focus, gathers our internal resources and allows us to access a state of being that did not exist until that moment. Once we make a decision to act upon something, we become one of those people who create the world that everyone else wakes up to in the morning. The world truly becomes ours.

The mind cannot tell the difference between an imagined and a real memory. Effectively, if we tell ourselves something often enough it will eventually seem as if it is true. Tell me, have you a memory of childhood? As you recall the memory, notice whether you can objectively see yourself in the memory itself. If so, it is not a real memory – how could it be? Can you see yourself doing things as if you were watching yourself right now? Yet we associate emotions with this memory and we have probably let it define our life experience in some way up to this point. It is not real but our mind has treated it as real and hence our behaviours.

The significance of this is that, no matter what may have occurred in the past, by choosing to make different decisions about the future we can change what has held us back in the past. Once we are masters of our decisions, we cannot continue to be victims of our past conditioning. Making a decision returns power to us. It lets us choose *action*. This action sets in motion a new dynamic which impacts on our experience and either confirms or changes the original conditioning.

A little story I usually tell my clients as a way of explaining this is about little Johnny, who starts off in life as a child whose mother hates dogs, absolutely abhors them as a result of a bad childhood experience of her own. So Johnny is *conditioned* by one of the most important people in his young life to have a set of *beliefs* about dogs based on this person's experience, not his. His beliefs are that dogs are bad and dangerous; his *feelings* are of hate and fear; his *attitude* can best be described as negative and this is what Johnny grows up with. He restricts his contact with dogs throughout his life in accordance with his learned beliefs and attitudes.

Then when Johnny gets to fourteen years of age, a dog unexpectedly jumps out in front of him on his way to school. All of a sudden his conditioning, beliefs, feelings and attitudes kick in and he *decides* to lash out and kick the dog for protection. As a result, the dog bites his leg. Through this one action Johnny has confirmed all his previous conditioning. Mom was right; dogs *are* bad.

However, let's imagine a different scenario, one in which Johnny has the same conditioning, beliefs, feelings and attitudes to the age of fourteen and is invited to call on the prettiest and most sought-after girl in the school after class one day. This is a biggie. If he manages to start dating this girl his popularity will soar and he will be the top guy in school – his reputation firmly established among his peers. He knocks on the door, she opens it…and sitting beside her is her favourite Alsatian dog, "Growler". The dog looks about seven feet tall and is looking at Johnny and growling, as if it is deciding which part to eat first. Johnny is faced with a problem. He could give in to all his previous conditioning and run like hell, in which case his life would be ruined, as she would tell all his friends how he ran screaming from "her little poochie". So, against every fibre of his being he decides to pet the dog. When he does the dog licks his hand and Johnny likes it! Now, his conditioning has been changed completely. Now not all dogs are bad and some can even be very nice!

Because Johnny associated a sense of great loss or gain from taking a specific action, which in ordinary circumstances he would not have done, his life is forever changed. For a coach a key part of the client intervention is helping the client identify what are the drivers that would encourage them to take actions that they may not have taken without such intervention. In this way, that which, in the past, may have held us back or reduced our ability to perform at a higher level can be changed and overcome.

So the Performance Loop (see page 26) indicates where a coach creates an intervention with their client and how they can change a great deal of the internal factors of performance for an individual by encouraging, supporting and challenging them to make bigger decisions and definite actions that lead to real change.

CONTINUOUS LEARNING AND IMPROVEMENT PROCESS

The last model, designed and introduced by Jonathan Bell, is the CLIP, or *Continuous Learning and Improvement Process*, which defines where coaching is placed within a learning organisation. There are five distinct phases to developing people in the learning organisation.

1. **Diagnosis**: identifying where the gap in performance is currently. For coaching, this is usually at an individual level and we use a psychometric profile evaluator to help determine this. The system we use currently is based on Jungian unconscious preferences. This evaluator uses 100 questions based on preferences within the workplace and then generates a report, which highlights communication, development and management preferences that we can use to effect

change at an individual level. We would also identify key motivators such as values, key performance indicators (KPI's) and the critical outcome for the client at this point.

2. **Education**: the formal learning process that adds knowledge to the process or transfers skills. Conducted either on a team or individual level, with a live facilitator or trainer, training provides the foundation from which all development will occur.

3. **Internalisation**: the use of audio/visual/interactive media to drive home the learning gained through formal training. We learn best through constant repetition and the convenience of having audio/visual material for repeat reference is a critical factor in the CLIP model. Such material should mirror the formal training taken by personnel and ease of access to relevant sections will encourage regular reviews of important material. We know that formal training will give us the key points that are relevant to us as we are taking the training – but having the option to review material as other areas become increasingly pertinent is a great support. With the increased commuting times now prevalent in major cities it is an opportunity to utilise downtime in the personal and professional development that would otherwise not be available.

4. **Implementation**: this is the phased and disciplined application of the knowledge and skills learned in pursuit of a specific objective. This is where the coach comes into the process, where the synergy that occurs within the coaching relationship can help clients accomplish more with the knowledge than they may have done alone. Implementation helps to continue and re-define the learning as a result of the experiences that

occur due to the dynamic set in motion through coaching. This is where it is useful to define training as education and coaching as the implementation of that knowledge. Training is education; coaching is implementation.

5. **Continuation**: while coaching continues the learning process on a one-to-one basis, it is useful to bring groups together on a regular basis to review previous material, introduce new knowledge and establish a company culture that is knowledge based, focused and applied to effect continuous performance improvement.

These are the key models we have developed to define or explain coaching and its place within a complete development programme. By giving a coachee a sense of where they are and why, and how they can look at continuous change, we initiate the empowerment of the individual.

Chapter Four

Core Beliefs of Coaching

There are a number of core concepts or beliefs about coaching that a professional coach does well to work by. The following are the most important beliefs that coaches and mentors might keep in mind when interfacing with their clients/team members and colleagues.

1. **Expectations: the coach should always expect more from the client than the client believes they are capable of accomplishing themselves.**

In coaching we are working towards a tangible change in both the performance and the personal perception of the client. To achieve this, it is necessary that the coach fully expects that the client is capable of accomplishing everything they set out to achieve. It is imperative that a coach/mentor believes that the client has all the resources they need to reach their goals, or can gain these resources on the journey of achievement that they are about to undertake. We need to believe this because our expectations of the person we are working with are subtly transmitted through both our voice tonality and body language. These two things alone make up 93 per cent of our total communication with others (1970 Study in Kinetics, University of Pennsylvania) and are unconsciously noticed and acted upon by our clients. How a coachee perceives our expectations of them will directly impact on their self-belief and their willingness to attempt what they have never achieved on their own in the past.

Our belief in others has an impact on ourselves too, on what is termed our "congruence". Congruence is that personal state when what we believe, feel and say all combine to create a powerfully credible communicative state that will always convince others of our sincerity in the process and our belief that they can successfully overcome past obstacles and power towards future success. Our expectations of the client, therefore, become the benchmark by which the client begins to change their assessment of themselves and raise their levels of self-expectation. This is the only way we can begin the process of increasing the Beta level of performance and start to shift perceptions that may have kept a person trapped in a limited performance cycle in the past.

Changing one's expectations is a critical factor in success. If success can be defined as "the achievement of pre-defined goals", then the impetus for being willing to create such goals comes from believing that by raising our personal expectations of ourselves, we can accomplish something more satisfying and valuable than what we possess at present. In short, if we allow our clients/staff to set standards that they have always set in the past, they will always get what they have got in the past.

Coaching exists to continuously create new standards of achievement and, therefore, a coach's expectations of clients' performance should always be more than what clients have accomplished prior to working with a coach. The willingness and the ability of the client to reach new standards begins with the conviction of the coach that they can make goals into dreams with a deadline.

2. **Compliance: clients should always feel engaged in the process.**

Compliance is a state of agreement between people, a willingness of one or the other to agree and work with the suggestions of others because they perceive a benefit from this. One could say it is the perfect state for an assertive person, who reaches their goals through persuasion and consultation rather than through direction and enforcement.

Effective coaches learn to create a situation of compliance with clients very quickly in the coaching relationship. Coaches are not there to give advice but to "ask questions and make suggestions". We are there to lead others to an understanding of their own personal power, not to prove how wonderful we are as advisors. The old adage "give a man a fish and you feed him for a day – teach him how to fish and you feed him for life" is especially true in the case of coaching. We need to quickly establish a relationship where coachees willingly comply with our suggestions. It is only when we have created this that we can effect real and lasting change for them. This is accomplished first by creating strong rapport between the coach and the client, which is in turn strengthened by the confidentiality aspect of coaching. This builds an atmosphere of trust and mutual respect between coach and client; an atmosphere where the client becomes more open to suggestions than they were prior to having a coach.

Compliance is also created by the clear understanding of the following: that the coach exists purely for the support of the coachee – to assist *them* to reach *their* agenda; that we as coach (or manager engaged in coaching) only reach *our* agenda by ensuring the client/team member reaches theirs; that coaches are intimately tied to the success of their clients; and that it is truly a relationship of *"Two-Minds and One Agenda"*.

So the clear definition of the coachee's agenda – their needs, desires and wants, and the successful elicitation of the values that motivate clients to drive towards these goals are critical elements in creating compliance.

3. **Global to Specific (G2S): breaking the inaction trance.**

Many people find themselves unable or unwilling to take action to change their circumstance because they view the challenge or problem in a global sense. They focus on the enormity of the challenge (and the global consequences of failure) rather than on the first thing they need to do to effect the change that would lead to the accomplishment of this same challenge. In coaching, our work is to help clients perceive such challenges and problems as surmountable via the completion of a succession of smaller activities. Once identified and sequenced properly, these activities are just smaller steps towards making the change they desire and achieving the greater goal.

Michael Gerber in his audio cassette, *The E-Myth*, mentions that extraordinary businesses are seldom created by extraordinary people. Rather, they are created by ordinary people who do the ordinary things extraordinarily well, mainly because good systems have been put in place that allow them to do this. Coaching is a system of excellence that helps us all achieve extraordinary things; a system that allows us all to soar towards our personal Alpha levels.

4. **Transparency: no hidden agendas.**

An important aspect of coaching, especially within a corporate context, is the existence of transparency in the process. By transparency I mean that both coach and client are working towards the same goal – the agenda of the client/staff member when allied to the overall objectives of the company. Coaching is a partnership and partners share things. The openness of the process assists rapport, trust and the free exchange of views and ideas that lead to a synergistic approach where all parties contribute. A simple example of this is the paperwork involved in coaching. The coach receives a copy of the same paperwork the client completes. Therefore, there is no information that both parties are not aware of. This is important because, in all circumstances, parity of esteem is paramount within coaching.

5. **Meaning: revealing the inner motivation.**

In coaching the existence of meaning is critical. This is the power that effects the greatest change in the client. As soon as the client finds a reason, a sense of purpose, then their own internal energies will drive the process and the coach simply acts as a guide and support, while the client moves inexorably towards the fulfilment of their needs. Once the coach has identified the real meaning and benefit in the process, their hard work is often over.

Working to one's values or personal meaning is essential for success: if there is a conflict in one's values then there is no progress. A huge number of people are striving for more meaning in their work but are unprepared to take the responsibility that comes with that – at least not on their own. Having a coach provides the support necessary to take on this responsibility and effect change in one's life and business. For those of us who wish to have more control over our lives and businesses, we must be willing to accept greater responsibility for the outcome of our actions. This is significantly easier and more focused when we have the help of a dedicated coach whose only agenda is our own.

6. Balance: managing the consequences of progress.

Even the most positive change requires a price, which we must all be willing to pay if we want to move from one place in life to another. For those who wish to reach more of their potential through coaching and reap the rewards that this brings with it, there can be substantial change, often in a very short period of time relative to what has happened before. How our family, friends and colleagues view us may change and we need to be prepared for that. Good coaches will encourage their clients to study the ecology of the consequences of their actions: what will they gain or lose by changing or accomplishing something? What will be required of them? What are they willing to do? And *then* what are they willing to do? Who are they really doing it for and why?

I often tell my clients that they stand on two legs: their professional leg and their personal leg. If either leg is weakened then the ability they have to move forward is greatly reduced. Therefore, it is important to look at all potential consequences and resolve them as best as is possible, so that our client can move forward confidently to new horizons.

7. 110 per cent: the least we can give.

If we are assisting people to be the very best that they can be, then as coaches we are bound to give everything that we have to help effect change. This is the 110 per cent contract that we should all enter into when coaching. It is not sufficient to do just enough in this profession; we should always do 10 per cent more than enough.

Giving 110 per cent is also in the coach's interest. There is probably no other business profession that requires such a deep and personal interest in the customer. After all, their success is directly related to our success: when they accomplish their objectives we will have played an integral part in that accomplishment.

Just like a coach who works with an athlete, business coaches are not the ones who win the gold medals. However, there can be a great sense of satisfaction when one reads or hears of a client or a colleague who has soared to new levels in their career as a result of our help. Most clients remember it too and it enhances our reputation, our earning power and our network of influence, ensuring our continued personal success from the success of others.

110 per cent – nothing less.

CHAPTER FIVE

A Code of Professional Ethics

Professional executive coaching, whether in sales, management or any other area of business, is a growing field. But there are, as yet, few standards. For those undertaking to venture into this new profession it may be useful to have a set of guidelines by which we conduct ourselves.

In this chapter I will outline my professional code of ethics, which all my coaching colleagues subscribe to. In our organisation, agreement to comply with this code of ethics is an essential part of contracts of employment.

First, I will outline the individual ethic and in some cases I will add some comments for further clarity.

1. **Coaches shall conduct coaching sessions at all times in a professional manner and in accordance with the code of conduct as outlined below.**

By "professional manner" I mean having respect for the client by arriving on time, dressed professionally and in a state of mind that is conducive to the best interest of the client.

2. **All matters between the coach and the client shall be treated as confidential. No third party shall have access to information given to the coach by the client. Exceptions to the above are (a) when the client has given permission in writing to divulge such information and (b) by force of law.**

I often bring this section to the attention of prospective clients. It can go a long way towards convincing them that they are dealing with someone who will protect their interest and watch over them. This can then help develop greater rapport. It helps to mention that nothing that occurs during the session will be repeated outside of the consulting room and that, as coaches, we are not here to make judgements. Therefore, they should feel free to discuss whatever they may feel has relevance to the process.

Because the coach is entirely objective, unlike our spouses, partners, business colleagues and so on, they tend not to be judgemental. As a result the coachee should feel relaxed enough to express whatever is relevant to the process. This gives the client permission to open up with information or feelings relevant to effecting change that may never have been brought to our attention without the security of the promise of confidentiality. The fact that they also have a say in who accesses the information, which requires their written permission, is reassuring and confirms their equal partnership in the process.

The section that covers the "force of law" is a requirement in the event of a client engaging in illegal activities. While we hope that this is unlikely ever to be invoked, nevertheless it can be used to protect our professional interests.

3. **The coach shall observe all laws, have a responsible manner in retaining the good name of coaches by attention to personal conduct, uphold the dignity and honour of the profession and accept its self-imposed disciplines.**

This section is self-explanatory but the relevance to self-imposed disciplines is worthy of mention. Because there are at present no agreed standards for coaching or its executive practice and because there are no agreed standards for the training and certification of such coaches, anybody can establish themselves in this area and create a business in this field, regardless of competency or experience. The guidelines indicated in Chapter 7, which address what to look for when buying-in coaching, will serve in some way to filter what has become a rash of coaching services. Unfortunately, in the immediate future, opportunities will remain for disreputable individuals to engage in this business and, therefore, it becomes important that reputable coaches agree to adhere to some form of self-imposed disciplines for good conduct.

Personally, I would welcome the formation of government recognised national or international institutes, which would assist in the direction and regulation of what I believe is an important 21st century profession. However, such institutes should not be run solely by people with academic credentials. Professional coaching needs to be pro-active in nature. Excessive academic qualifications – as opposed to the ability of coaches to be multi-disciplined in creativity, experience, thinking skills, planning, lateral thinking, communications and all the other disciplines that make a good coach – would only remove the very essence of this emerging field.

4. **Coaches should avoid dual relationships with clients and should never offer their services under terms or conditions that might impair the free and complete exercise of their professional judgement and skill, and reduce the quality of their service or risk exploitation.**

In short, the coach/client relationship is paramount.

Therefore, ideally, a coach should have no personal relationship with a client other than that of a business or professional nature.

While coaching is not therapy and, therefore, the same emotions that are unleashed in the therapeutic environment should not be present, there is always the strong possibility of transference and counter-transference between coach and client. Transference is the phenomenon where there are strong emotional bonds/attractions created from the client to the coach. Counter-transference is where the same emotional attachments/attractions are created from coach to client. While coaching functions with a level of a relationship between coach and client that is entirely dependent on excellent rapport, trust and the willingness to listen and to co-create new futures, clearly there is a level of involvement that may not be appropriate and would hinder a coach doing their job for the client effectively. In short, if there is a desire to have a personal relationship outside the consulting room it is often better to pass the client to another coach, so that their best interests continue to be served.

One further point. Coaches work for a professional fee. They should not work for a percentage of the client's business. In the event of a client seeking to invite a coach into the business, the professional coaching relationship should cease, as the coach is no longer an impartial agent.

5. **The coach shall keep up to date with material and innovation in their specific field and in fields of a related nature to ensure that best practice is applied at all times.**

Coaches need to continually keep abreast of developments in the coaching field and in the fields of management, sales and business thinking that relate to their chosen area of speciality. This allows them to bring the best of information to the coaching process at all times. In short, professional coaches should commit to the principle of life-long learning, using every opportunity to expand their knowledge and the resources that they can bring to their clients.

We should commit to the principle of self-actualisation as it pertains to us. New knowledge and new experiences are the stock-in-trade of a professional executive coach. They allow us to continually evolve so that the services we then provide are always at the highest possible level and guarantee the principle of 110 per cent.

6. **Prior to entering into a professional relationship the coach must ensure that the nature of coaching, the purpose of coaching, the anticipated length of coaching and the cost of the coaching service has been disclosed to the client. No service is to be entered into until an informed consent has been secured from the client.**

Caveat Emptor or "buyer beware" has no place in coaching: the client must understand fully the commitment of both coach and client to the process. We offer a one-hour complimentary session, within which we explain the models involved, give the client a direct experience of the process through an exercise called the "Coaching Trinity" and then outline the financial and time commitments that the client is taking on board. The client must be the judge of the value of the service: an informed judgement makes the process more effective and the results more immediate.

7. **Coaches will not engage in the provision of advice**

of a marital or financial nature or in any field in which they are not professionally qualified. They and their clients must acknowledge that coaching is a process of setting objectives, identifying obstacles, mutually agreeing and co-designing solutions, and implementing actions that are consistent with improving the professional performance of the client (see section 8).

Strictly speaking, coaches do not give advice – we ask questions and make suggestions. Any advice we do give should be relevant to the field of knowledge that we possess and, even then, it should be couched as a question, so that the client may give due consideration to the suggestion. While we need to consider that life balance, the ecology of planning and the personal aspect play a part in professional objectives and performance, we should not be there to act as therapists and counsellors. There is a level at which it is not appropriate to engage with the personal concerns of the client – especially if we have not been professionally trained to do so.

8. **If during the course of coaching, information is disclosed that would suggest a referral or consultation with another professional would be appropriate, the coaching shall be terminated and the client encouraged to make suitable alternative professional arrangements.**

It is not something coaches are likely to encounter very often, if at all, but if, during coaching, a client should indicate through their demeanour or language that there are deeper issues at work and that therapy might be required, the simple rule is this: *if in doubt, refer it out.*

Suggest to the client that there may be issues that they need to resolve before continuing with the process and that this would only help the process further. Be willing to suspend the coaching process and promise the client that they can return to the process when they have had a consultation with the professional they are referred to.

9. **A coach shall maintain a duty of care towards clients and shall terminate their relationship with a client when the client can no longer benefit from continued service and shall not provide service if they do not in good faith believe that the client will benefit from the service provided.**

Coaching exists to enhance the performance of clients. In doing so, it should attempt to improve the self-reliance and self-dependency of the client. It should not be about creating dependent clients who feel that without the coach they can accomplish nothing. Usually, the most intensive contact between the coach and the client exists at the commencement of the relationship. After this, it should be sufficient to offer less intensive continuation programmes that will help us to maintain the foundations of good pro-activity and performance.

While dependent clients might sound like a great business idea, it would in due course serve the coach nothing. As coaches we avoid burnout partly by being stimulated by the challenge of new faces and new worlds to help create. This is enshrined in section 10.

10. **The coach should keep in mind at all times that the underlying purpose of coaching is to create improved client performance through creating self-reliance rather than dependency and should**

maintain the best interests of the client and the profession at all times.

CHAPTER SIX

The Tools of Coaching

So what are some of the critical tools that we use when coaching? What is it that allows us to effect such significant change in people over a short period of time? There are two areas I would like to review. The first set of tools is what one might call the *"intangibles"* and the second set is the *"tangibles"*.

The intangibles are used to create the coaching environment and the tangibles are then used to help to focus the often "global" concerns of a client into specific, actionable concerns and define the actual process of coaching.

THE INTANGIBLES

Rapport

Rapport is that indefinable quality that makes or breaks a business or personal relationship. It is often something that is considered an unconscious and hence indefinable process but its importance in any form of relationship is immense. Whether it is a doctor's bedside manner, a friend's obvious respect and concern for us, or a colleague's commitment to a shared vision, rapport plays a huge part in healing, commitment and accomplishment. No more so than in coaching, where the coach must create an environment in which the client feels sufficiently safe and able to share issues and personal perspectives, which the coach must interact with to effect a change in performance.

To date, we have effected a significant study into rapport because of its importance in the field of human interaction and it is an area of high priority for coaches in training. We spend quite some time on helping our coach "trainees" become proficient at creating rapport in any environment. While it is obviously a quality we all have to a greater or lesser extent, only creating rapport unconsciously is not sufficient in a professional relationship such as in sales or coaching.

It is the responsibility of the sales professional or coaching professional to create rapport with volition, or by choice, with anyone they encounter. I define rapport as *that **state** in human relations where there is an **agreed**, sometimes silent, **recognition** and **acceptance** of **common issues***. It is a state or feeling shared by two people of mutual understanding and respect. Within the coaching relationship, rapport comes from what should be the coach's obvious desire for and expectation of higher things for their client and a common purpose of accomplishing a shared dream – the client's dream, the accomplishment of which the coach plays a critical role in effecting. Things such as body language and posture, breathing, the use of the client's words and language, the opportunities for physical touch such as handshakes all play a part in creating a safe, secure and confident environment for the client who is about to undergo a process of change.

Change is a formidable task and the first step in encouraging such change is to create a protected environment and then proceed with small steps in a sequential process. Rapport is the key tool that allows the creation of such a change-orientated environment.

"Soft" Language

Matching of a client's language and vocabulary is important in coaching because it is how clients express what is meaningful to them. Words, at best, are inadequate at expressing the full range of our experiences. The meaning they convey is important, however, and so our coaches are trained to use the client's positive language to establish rapport and encouragement, and to re-frame (or change) a client's negative language. For example, we seldom allow our clients to use the word "try" because when this word is used it becomes a code for failure. "I'll try" might as well be "it won't be done" because inherent in the word is the fact that insufficient effort to effect change will be applied – but at least "I tried". So the client must create a clear statement of intent around their work before they get away from a session.

It is perfectly acceptable, however, for a coach to use the word "try" when encouraging the client to try something completely different from their past experiences. This is because even an attempt that fails will help the process of altering the client's perspective on the benefits of a new approach.

But "soft" language is something more again. In the past, management language was directive: "do this, do that, this must be done, effect it immediately, get it done, you must/have to do this". This resulted in fear- /threat-based motivation, which, at best, was only short term.

Short-term motivation needs constant re-installing in staff. In time it creates resistance and even resentment. The benefit of coaching within the organisation is that it creates employee-centred management where employees are willing to invest more of themselves in their work. The language used when creating this needs to be softer, more expansive and inclusive, and is generally couched in questions: "Have you *considered*...? "*If* we were to...?" Where *might* we find...?" "*How would* this be best viewed...?" "If we *were* to look at things differently...?" "*Assuming* that this was possible what would you do first...?" It often involves changing tenses, possibilities and assumptions, identifying and attaching meaning, and the use of what we call the "**inclusive WE**". The "inclusive WE" is more properly referred to as "forced teaming", where the coach immediately begins to speak using the referential index "WE", implying that both coach and client are now working on the client's goals as a team. The coach would only return to using "you" where the client is being tied down to a specific action. Using "WE" rapidly installs in the client the idea that they are not alone in reaching for these new heights; that now they are being paced, assisted, encouraged and involved in a process of accountability that they have volunteered to be a part of for their own betterment.

Attitude

The attitude of the coach is another important intangible in the process. The coach must:

- be non-judgemental
- be optimistic
- have total conviction in the success of the partnership and the ability of the client to effect the desired change
- encourage an environment of trust by being willing to share relevant personal experience
- be committed to the transparency of the process
- be willing to commit whatever personal resources they

have to the success of their client

• have a "full-on" focus on the client.

The client's success should be paramount to the coach. It demands a great deal from us but there is a great deal of satisfaction in seeing a client become more of themselves through their involvement with us.

THE TANGIBLES

The tangibles are the specific tools we use when coaching. In defining them, I have also identified the actual coaching process used by coaches trained by our company.

Questions

Coaching begins and ends with questions. In coaching questions are used to encourage dialogue, relax the client and create a conversational environment. However, they have more specific purposes too.

To install ideas

Questioning the client engages them in the process and as a result they are highly attentive. While they are in this attentive state, it is useful to be able to make suggestions which are then taken on board by the client, more willingly than if we were to instruct or direct them. For example, "Imagine a situation where the problem was resolved and we found ourselves to be more successful, that would be worth taking a small risk for, wouldn't it?" or "Although in the past this may have been difficult, if we were to look at things differently for the future, how might we start making changes?"

Within these questions we are also using "framing" to put a context – such as "in the past" – on the question, leaving previous difficulties where they belong and encouraging the client to take a different approach now.

To change perspectives and give instructions

"If we were to see a new way of doing the job more effectively, where might we make a start?" Within this question we have encouraged the client to look at their job differently. We have also automatically assumed that they will do this (a function of expectation). If the client had queried this we would express surprise and re-state the question, firmly placing them in a pro-active mode, and instruct them to reply with new answers.

To help reach compliance

Compliance is the ideal coaching state. It is where the client is willing to "try on" suggestions that in any other context of management they might consider too personal, too directive or even too difficult to attempt. Because questions help us to engage the client in "the game", they also convey ownership of the process to them. We become co-conspirators, facilitators and guides. A client should seldom get a direct answer from a coach. We don't give advice; we just make suggestions. We never make statements when a question will ensure greater client understanding, ownership and hence compliance.

In our coaching we have created a trio of questions, which begin the process of coaching with all clients. I have called them the *Coaching Trinity*. The first of these identifies the most important issue the client is currently facing:

> *At the present time, what is the greatest challenge*
> *that you're facing in the job?* or, to restate it, *What*
> *one thing could we do that, when done, would effect*
> *the greatest amount of change in your job or career?*

Once the client has defined the issue, the answer to this
first question often needs to be explored further by sub-
questions. For example, we would seek to create a concise
and specific objective from their answer. The language we
use in defining this objective is very important, as it must
be positively framed, personal and specific. The exact
language the coach uses with the questions might vary
depending on the type of client or the level of employee
you are working with. It is essential that we use the client's
language – but often clients can get "stuck" in specifying
the objective's language. If this is the case, we must assist
them in structuring this first and most important objective.
A coach would then seek to *identify the meaning* or the
passion the client would attach to reaching this goal by
asking something like:

> *What specifically would this do for you personally,*
> *and I don't mean within the job, I mean for you*
> *personally? What would be different for you as a*
> *result of having this happen?*

Having identified this, we have now found a structured,
written objective with a clear, personal, written benefit for
its accomplishment attached. It is the one thing that would
fundamentally change the client's world as it is at the
present.

We now move to the second question:

> *What are the things you would love to do in the job?*

> *Things that you would really enjoy doing and that could bring some real benefit to your work/position/ job?*

Now we are identifying the things that would really motivate the client and effect real change in their current environment (and hence their perception of that environment). This is where we identify the "extra" things that the client is willing to do to improve their performance and gain significant personal satisfaction as a result. At this point, we are addressing the things that clients often promise themselves but seldom accomplish on their own. It is here that we start to close the performance gap.

The third question is designed to clear the decks, to take everything that should be addressed to the fore and ensure that the client's focus is always on that which will effect the greatest change.

> *What sort of things are we deferring or putting on the long finger that there is no need to defer anymore? Make a complete list of even the smallest things. Let's now get them out of the way.*

Out of these questions we have by now assembled a list of things that are of most importance to the client at this moment in time. Now we will ask them to review that list, first highlighting with a marker the four most important projects on the list and only then sequencing them in order. Colour and sequence are important factors in creative thinking. Now we have the material for future performance improvement and by now we should also have the client's buy-in to the process. Next we have to process the material.

The Objectives Sheet

The objectives sheet is stage two of the coaching process. This is what we use to further specify the critical client objectives and the meaning that they attach to their accomplishment.

Part one of the sheet requests a definition of each of the objectives/meanings that the client is aiming for.

Part two of the sheet then asks the client to define what obstacles may have held them back "in the past". The use of the phrase "in the past" is important as it indicates to the staff member or client that we are attaching no blame to the lack of accomplishment to date. We are also implying that now we can move forward towards accomplishing these objectives in the future. In addition, should we fail to have the obstacles clearly defined and placed on paper where we can control them, we run the risk of having the obstacles remain within the client's thinking as ill-defined anxieties or belief-saboteurs.

Part three of the objectives sheet is a listing of the sort of skills or resources that the client wishes to take from the coaching process. In effect, we are asking how they would like to be changed as a result of the process. We have also restored the client to a positive state of anticipation of the outcome of coaching, after they have just taken time to identify what has previously held them back. We always want the client thinking about where they want to be – not where they have been.

The Meta View

The Meta View is an exercise used to change the client's perception of time and to help them to be convinced that the objectives they have outlined are reachable. There are two Meta views: the Meta View 5 and the Meta View 1, for five years hence and one for a single year from now respectively.

Because of the longer period of time involved, the Meta View 5 encourages the client to think beyond current boundaries. The Meta View 1 is simply an essay about the next 12 months. It is designed to focus the Meta View 5 thinking more specifically. We want the client to write about how things will be different as a result of accomplishing their objectives through coaching: what will have changed? How did it change? When was the change first noticed? We want them to be as specific as possible.

The Meta View exercise is based on the understanding that the mind cannot tell the difference between real and imagined memories. As a result of getting the client to write the exercise, the coach has now helped instill the following into the client's thinking:

- that the objectives are "do-able"

- a clear picture of the benefits to be gained

- that their behaviours and expectations can start the change necessary to allow them to accomplish the goals.

The mind supposedly deletes, distorts and generalises information. With a "guestimated" data-input of 2,000,000 items per second, the mind must adopt prioritisation procedures to process only the information most relevant to the brain. Through this exercise the client is ensuring that the relevant information will be recognised and fed through to their consciousness so that they act upon it. We call this exercise "creative re-programming" or "switching on the synchronicity". A subsequent part of the exercise also allows us to access the critical areas of importance to the client – which we can then use to motivate them as necessary.

The SMART Goal

Once we identify the critical issues, we break them down even further through the use of SMART goals. Most people are familiar with the idea of SMART goals – language should be simple and specific, the goal measurable and meaningful, written in the present tense and so forth. The important points are: that the major goals should be broken down into smaller actions; that a clear picture of the outcome of the goal is generated; and that there is a date by when it should be accomplished. Several goals may be defined, covering diverse areas – depending on what is defined as important by the client.

The Action Plan

The Action Plan sheet is used as the tool by which the client is focused on what they need to be doing to effect the change they are looking for. This sheet itemises the actions necessary to move forward and may include different actions from different SMART goals. The sheet is dated and signed by the client and becomes the means by which the client is held accountable for their actions during later coaching sessions.

An important point to note is that we have our clients date each individual action. I discovered quite early on that clients who did not have each action dated often returned to sessions having accomplished less than they did when we had them deadline each action. It brought a greater sense of urgency to the process.

After a number of sessions, one may find that the client

has exhausted all the actions they originally defined through their SMART goals. This is not a problem, because if they have accomplished the earlier actions they will have now created a "dynamic" that will help carry them to their ultimate goal.

How the action plan is handled is also important. When the client has accomplished an action they are encouraged to place a "tick" beside the action – a visual and emotive anchor back to school days when they got a correct answer. If an action has not been accomplished then we *do not* place an "X" mark beside it, as this may be a visual and emotive anchor back to a negative feeling. Instead we circle the number of the action and discuss where the client experienced difficulty. In cases where a client has not acted on a specific action, for at least two sessions, then we may need to challenge the client. In this case it is useful to ask "just how important" is this to the client (and lose it or keep it accordingly) or to ask them if we need to break it down further to make it more easily accomplished.

Clients often get an early buzz from the fact that they are making real change. Coaches can use this "buzz" to remind clients of how much more useful it is to be pro-active when facing challenges and (of course!) how beneficial it is to be working with a coach who helps them accomplish personal excellence through partnership.

Timing of Sessions

Usually professional coaching sessions last about 60 to 90 minutes and sessions are arranged every five or ten working days. When a client starts with us for the first time, they are usually expected to complete approximately eight initial sessions – a mixture of live sessions and telephone sessions lasting about 30 minutes. In the company environment, the number of sessions will depend on the response of the staff member. If the member is responding well they may only need to have "formal" sessions once every two/four weeks. If they are not responding well, and are obviously in need of greater support, then the coach/manager may decide to work with them on a weekly basis.

In this chapter, we have analysed some of the main tools in a professional coach's armoury – both the tangibles and the intangibles of coaching. Used correctly and with the right balance, they can effect massive change for our clients.

CHAPTER SEVEN

Introducing Coaching into Organisations

When introducing coaching into an organisation there are a number of factors that need to be considered: at what level is coaching brought in initially? Where is it best positioned? What are the procedures for vetting suppliers of coaching services? What challenges will it create for existing managers? What do we do when we face resistance? What happens if there is a conflict of interest between the objectives of the person being coached and the company's objectives for them? This chapter will act as a guide to answering some of these questions.

Coaching is best positioned with the senior management team. The benefits of senior personnel working with a coach are significant, as an improvement in the quality of their performance has significant effects on the rest of the organisation. Many senior managers often exist in a position of isolation, with enormous pressures for results. They are constantly aware of "the positioning and profile issues" inherent at senior company level and the effect that they can have on future promotion.

An external professional, whose sole purpose is to bring an intervention that will assist the executive to reach their objectives, can be a valuable resource, a springboard to generate ideas, a person to help them take time to reflect, plan for the future, structure their thinking and launch new initiatives. This situation also gives the executive an immediate understanding of the effect that the coaching process can have on their own managers and teams, thereby enlisting them successfully in what becomes a cultural shift in the organisation.

However, it is not always possible to access senior management and, therefore, to establish a coaching beach head one might start with the human resource department. In many cases they will have an understanding of coaching, if not the intricacies of the process, and will be able to assist buy-in by critical middle managers. HR managers are often the first clients that join from companies, as they see the benefits that coaching can bring in helping them reach their own professional objectives. Alternatively, sales directors and sales managers are excellent initial points of contact as they are charged with delivering on the most critical of business functions. Being such a dynamic process, sales is an area that readily lends itself to performance improvement through coaching. The tangible financial return that coaching can bring with performance improvement can be especially attractive.

CHOOSING A COACHING PROVIDER

Buying-in coaching from a potential supplier is often an area that needs to be carefully considered. Coaching has rapidly evolved as a "buzzword" over the last few years. It is often perceived as being just a fad. But coaching is here to stay and, therefore, the coaching provider that an organisation commits to partner with for the provision of coaching needs to be carefully scrutinised.

First, is it actually a coaching practice, or a training company, that sells "coaching" as a means of getting a hearing from us? Too many companies are just so – that is, they are not dedicated business coaching practices. This is important, as this is the company that will interface with many of our key staff, develop relationships with them and assist them with performance improvement. If they are qualified to do this correctly, we can be sure of an excellent service, making a real difference to our organisation. To confirm the bona fides of a potential supplier we might ask the following questions:

1. Do you have a professional Code of Ethics that defines your relationship between the coach and the client?

2. Do you have current professional indemnity insurance?

3. Who are the companies you are currently working with? What industries are they from? At what level are you coaching? What specific areas are you qualified to coach in?

4. What is your training? How are you certified to coach?

5. What models is your coaching based upon?

6. Do you have clients who will speak for you and can we have their names and contact numbers?

7. Are you willing to provide a complimentary session as a means of assessing your skills?

8. What does your coaching programme consist of? What materials are provided?

9. Over what time period is the coaching being provided? Is there a definitive start and end date?

If the potential provider is willing to answer the above to our satisfaction, then we can consider them as a supplier. Once the supplier is chosen and agreed upon, we can then begin the process of introducing coaching to the company.

The establishment of a coaching culture within an organisation can bring a number of potential benefits for that organisation. Listed below are just four key benefits.

1. Coaching Delivers on Training

Unlike training, which is primarily an educational function, coaching (in the guise of mentoring) is essentially an implementation function. It is about using the knowledge gained in the training and applying it to effect change. Today's corporate training budgets are sometimes less effective for the want of the support and supervision that would help to ensure the application of coaching. "Sheep dipping" (the placement of large numbers of candidates on formal trainings in the hope that some might stick) can be a common training policy used by management wishing to be seen to be acting on company problems. Even with good training, the benefits are often lost when the delegate returns to their original environment where, with no further support, the training manual goes on the top shelf to gather dust, never to be looked at again.

However, when a delegate is coached over a period of time after completing a training, the effective use of that learning is significantly increased and the net gain from the training investment to the organisation greatly enhanced. Coaching can, in this case, be considered to deliver what training alone can often only promise. There may be a case to be made that the training departments in organisations should be tasked not only with the provision of training, but with the implementation of that training through regular coaching practice, in association with management. Here their specific expertise can be used, together with the normal coaching of the manager, to mentor the delegate to higher standards of performance in the area in which they have been trained. Alternatively, the training department becomes a centre of coaching resources within the organisation that is able to provide coaching, as required, to support line managers.

2. Coaching Builds and Maintains Relationships

In the past, traditional management methods did not encourage close relationships between managers and staff. Management was a directive approach, with managers trained to focus on what staff did poorly rather than on what they did well. Such a focus often failed to create a collaborative approach to business and instead produced one that played a large part in the "them or us" perspective – a divisive and often self-defeating approach.

Today a more collaborative approach is desired based on creating partnership between managers and team members. The emphasis is on co-operation, on utilising the resources and insights of all members of the team. The objective is to create a unique synergy between management and staff that will lead teams to new and more inclusive ways of team management and development. The manager now coaches his team members to their potential and harnesses that inherent potential to meet team objectives.

To encourage team members to explore those hidden resources the manager must be able to build open relationships with his team members. There can be no hidden agendas and no power trips. Effective coaching practice places particular emphasis on the relationship between management and teams. It bases its success on the level of rapport, trust and communication that can be built to create a harmonious and pro-active work environment where, ideally, everyone is acknowledged for their contribution.

This is often challenging for the manager, as they must now be willing to get closer to staff than before – so close that staff may see their weaknesses and flaws. However, in a coaching environment, such flaws are more acceptable. With the manager acting as coach, it is the combined strengths of the team that matter. The most important factors are the positive resources of all contributors that help the team meet its objectives.

Time spent dealing with problems can now be reduced, as the coaching relationship allows feedback to be given directly after an event and in an environment of mutual development, rather than mutual suspicion. The effect of this is to reduce time-wasting personnel issues, another significant contribution to company health and welfare.

In a coaching culture, the traditional form of management by punishing mistakes is replaced by a more positive feedback process, one where both the knowledge of the manager and the event-specific learning of the staff member can be harmonised into more effective work practice.

3. Coaching Fosters Self-Reliance and Solution-Oriented Thinking

The strength of coaching is that it offers a systematic process that harnesses the unique strengths of individuals, focused through the coach, to create a solution-orientated and pro-active environment. In such an environment, people are happy to contribute because they are being recognised and assisted towards their needs through the work that they are doing. Because more meaning is attached to the work, responsibility can be more widely dispersed within the team. I call this *"autonomy through co-operation"*, as with team members now more willing to initiate, the manager is now in a position to delegate further and with greater confidence.

The result is not only increased individual contributions from team members, who now feel that they have a voice in the direction and the results of the team, but also the fact that the manager can now work more strategically on the team's goals. The benefits of releasing a skilled manager from having to constantly double-check on their staff is considerable, as the manager may now function on their primary task of having the team meet company objectives.

4. Consistency in Management Style

Managers learn most of their skills initially through consciously or unconsciously modelling the behaviour of their own managers. They take on board management habits for good or ill. Add to this management training and their own personality and we have a model of management that can be determined by the conditioning and personality of the individual manager. This can sometimes lead to an inconsistency in the manager's performance and the operational performance of the individuals that they manage. Many companies have standards that they expect managers to adhere to but the problem can be that, with the stress created by more demands in less time, most managers often attempt to get the job done as they see fit.

Coaching can be a simple and systematic process of management. It follows certain easy-to-follow guidelines, it has a specific outcome in mind and it creates an environment where all outcomes can be accomplished within a realistic time frame. It does not look to the manager to see the work completed but to the individual employee, charging them with a personal reason to see it completed. It employs both formal and informal meetings as part of its structure. Once the coaching process is employed, it creates effective performance and brings consistency in management style.

With such a standard methodology, a staff member transferring between departments or teams can be managed in exactly the same way as in their previous department. To a great extent, this removes the effect of management personality from the equation, reducing the new team member's learning curve and helping them to contribute more in a shorter period of time.

Areas where coaching might successfully be applied include:

• temporary assignments

• after training programmes

• special projects

• new jobs or promotion

• planned delegation

• problems and successes.

CHALLENGES TO INTRODUCING COACHING INTO ORGANISATIONS

Introducing business coaching into an organisation can also create challenges that need to be met in order to effectively implement successful coaching processes. Let's now consider what some of these challenges might be.

Rapid change is a feature of modern business. Business is driven by the next new process or idea and the ability to respond quickly to market forces is the brand of successful businesses. However, it can be easy to overlook the fact that all change is both driven and managed by people – and that the pace of change is different for everyone. Some people are pro-active: they create the world in which we live; they look to the next challenge, the next opportunity. Many others are reactive: slow to change; fearful of losing what it is they now hold.

This fear of change can be ingrained in our organisations as well. Some organisations adapt quickly and respond to challenges with enthusiasm. For the many who fail to do so effectively, part of the problem is the speed and manner with which information is transmitted through the organisation. They lack the flexibility necessary to adapt quickly. This can be seen most clearly in the relationship between management and staff. Organisations that are "institutionalised" – where information is used as a means of control, where highly defined hierarchal reporting structures are adhered to, where seniority is prized over merit, where academic excellence is rated over delivered performance, where old stereotypes are allowed to dominate in the face of the changing nature of the workforce – these organisations face the greatest challenge. In such organisations, managers have the greatest fear of change and hence the greatest resistance to the idea of a coaching culture, which they see as a threat to their established and rigid management style, and the authority they exert over their staff. Yet these same organisations are haemorrhaging their best people, who opt to leave for organisations that embrace a more open and synergistic management approach that will allow them to fulfil their potential.

The imagined fear of loss as a result of the introduction to coaching, this fear of personal exposure to staff, the greater intimacy and the risks associated with that, are challenges when introducing coaching processes to certain organisations. Fortunately, when we train managers in coaching skills they are assisted in facing these concerns through a series of steps, which allow them to prepare their teams for this new style of approach. One of these steps is the initial team meeting where coaching is introduced, critical performance indicators are identified and then allocated to team members. This team meeting not only defines the new parameters but also benchmarks the team through their own feedback as to how the team views its current performance. For the manager, regularly exposed to group meetings, it is a painless way of implementing the initial stages of coaching: from this meeting comes the first stage in creating team/coach synergy and mutual agreement. It is also the first step that ensures they can guide the objectives of the individual in line with the company objectives. In all cases, coaching is designed to create a quantifiable and measurable change in business performance.

The follow-on from this meeting is to use the agreed benchmarks as a means of identifying performance targets for an individual team member. This then leads to the first of the one-to-one meetings, which begin the process of coaching at a level with which the manager may feel comfortable. From the individual meeting will come proposed actions that the staff member co-designs with their coach, which will positively impact on their performance and have a high degree of personal meaning for them.

When this point has been reached coaching has begun. All that is necessary now is to maintain the discipline of the process through agreed formal meetings at set intervals for the purpose of feedback and re-focusing.

All change comes from action and the smaller the action the easier it is to get agreement to begin. Motivation and generating self-esteem in team members is something that evolves from them through the successful accomplishment of defined activities. In commencing coaching, managers are encouraged to start small, for themselves and their team members. They are encouraged to start with the most co-operative/friendly of staff members. Mistakes will be made at the start and the most forgiving of people are the ones to start with. This allows a manager to build up their confidence in the process.

Managers are often surprised at the initial euphoric buzz that many team members get when coaching begins. This is often because, for the first time, employees are actively contributing and feel that they have some ownership of the process. This does subside but what managers then find is that many employees start to drive the process itself, raising their own personal standards and suggesting new initiatives and ideas. It is then necessary for the manager to maintain the discipline, the clear focus and re-focusing, and the positive feedback to the staff members that are necessary.

In a large financial services company, which applied our methods of coaching, the following story was told to us by a senior manager. He had attended a social function for one of his teams. The team leader had recently been trained in coaching principles and had been applying it for a short time with the team. This team had also just been joined by two new recruits from outside the organisation. At the function the senior manager had met with the new recruits and asked them how they were finding their first weeks with the team. "It's wonderful," replied one. "I've never worked with a company before where a team leader actually talks to you!"

Another challenge to introducing coaching is the need
for the manager to maintain the coaching discipline until
it is second nature – until it is the *process* of management
rather than merely a competency thereof. Coaching requires
discipline. To be successful, it is necessary that discipline
be applied systematically. In the early stages, its success
will hinge on the disciplined application of the coaching
process. This is not always easy. One of our greatest
challenges is convincing managers that if, despite the time
pressures they are already working under, they take some
additional time at the start to ensure that the process
becomes a regular and expected one, they will save hours
of time and years of stress.

Part of the means by which we encourage the
development of an organisation's culture from directive to
consultative and by which we support trained managers is
to encourage the formation of *coaching forums*. These
forums consist of a group of managers, selected from those
who have completed training, brought together to chart
the development of coaching in the organisation. They meet
regularly for the purpose of:

- discussing the effect of coaching within the organisation

- discussing new ideas or initiatives that have evolved from
the workforce as a result of coaching

- supporting individual managers in the discipline of its
application, taking further training in relevant skills

- developing an internal code of ethics

- briefing senior management on coaching's effects in the
workplace and so forth.

In all cases coaching from an external management source
to a large organisation should be seen only as a catalyst –

an organisation's first step towards developing its own approach to the use of coaching. An organisation should be encouraged to create its own body of learning and coaching style. In an ideal world, an outside agency should remain involved at only two levels after the management team has been trained: first, to provide a coaching service to the most senior members of the management team, who would not be willing to be coached by more junior managers; secondly, to provide ongoing support to the internal coaching forum on further developments in coaching or relevant skills.

Challenges to coaching can arise when an individual is facing redundancy or retirement. How can one encourage such staff to engage in the process? The answer lies in how skilfully the manager/coach can harmonise what is most important to the individual – retirement or redundancy – with what is expected of them for their remaining time in the company. As long as people can see a direct personal benefit from their actions, they can be coached.

We are often asked, "Can everybody be coached?" Theoretically, the answer is "Yes". But realistically there will always be a percentage of people that confounds the theory. Therefore, in the event that, for whatever reason, a team member resolutely resists coaching – walk away, do not coach them. Coaching should be seen as a means of "fast-tracking" people, a positive resource that allows a team member to actively engage in an affirmative and personal way with the management and success of their team. If somebody refuses to co-operate they should no longer have access to that resource. In our experience, it is often the case that, as the rest of the team benefits from a different management approach and a more positive work environment, most reluctant employees can be won around.

In this case there is also one other point worth noting.

We need to be careful that it is not *our* expectation or pre-judgement of a staff member's willingness to be coached that is the problem. As a manager, we will have a history with certain team members when it comes to introducing coaching. It is useful to remember that coaching can be a new start for both manager and team, and is limited only by our level of expectation of the team. It has been repeatedly shown that staff will rise to our expectations of them.

A branch manager of a building society who had taken our training was not looking forward to introducing his new-found skills to his team. He had worked with them for seven years and felt that he knew them well. He worried that he would face resistance to this new thinking, specifically from a particular person who had been with the organisation many years more than he. However, he persevered with the coaching process, starting with the team meeting and bringing it down to a one-to-one basis. To his surprise, he found that the staff were delighted with this new personal approach, that their performance levels soared and that they took greater responsibility for initiatives within the branch. He was right to expect resistance from this one individual. However, as they saw the change in the branch and in their co-workers, as they noticed that people were delivering on promises, in the end they too entered the process. Much to the manager's surprise, once this person had embraced the process, they became an invaluable source of knowledge and experience, subsequently responsible for performance-enhancing ideas that were applied throughout the branch network.

For us as coaches, helping others overcome the challenge of their limiting expectations can reap significant rewards. Experienced coaches know that they can be very conversational in their approach and therefore can go a long way towards reaching the buy-in that they require from someone being coached before it becomes obvious that a specific process is at work. However, for various reasons, coaches sometimes face resistance to coaching and a person may not be willing to involve themselves in the process. At this point a coach may need to fall back on their ability to gain compliance through ascertaining the values of a person and using them to create powerful reasons for that person to engage in the process. People are usually motivated by personal pleasure, so the coaching process can be presented as a system that brings personal benefit to the individual. This is best accomplished by eliciting the individual's values and applying them to the benefits the process can bring to an individual.

Values are abstract concepts, such as money, promotion, fulfilment and so on, that motivate us *towards* an objective or *away* from an objective. As a simple example take someone who says they want to be rich. "Why is that important to you?" we might ask, to which question the response might be, "So that I can care for my family and have a good time." This is a *toward* response as it helps focus the client and their actions on creating a new situation that is positive. However, we might ask someone else why they wish to be rich and the response might be, "So that I'm not poor." In this instance, the person's motivation is to "get away from" a negative situation. This negative motivation is usually short term and quickly fades when the person has gained distance from the situation they wish to avoid. As a result, is it useless for consistent performance improvement. Therefore, it is necessary for a coach to have the person identify what are the benefits they can gain from engaging with coaching. Language, and the meaning attached to it, is an important issue for both client and practitioner. Using the right words can have a significant effect on a person's performance.

Let's look at the process used when we seek to gain motivation through values elicitation.

1. The most effective method of overcoming resistance to coaching at an individual level is to attach a significant degree of personal meaning to the process.

2. People are usually motivated by personal pleasure and so the coaching process can be presented as a system that brings personal benefit to the individual.

3. This is best accomplished by eliciting the individual's values and applying them to the benefits the process can bring to the individual.

4. As we may know, values are abstract concepts, which have a motivational direction and are sequenced in a particular order, from which our beliefs about our potentials and ourselves are grounded.

Values are elicited as follows:

1. In the most conversational way possible, ask the person "In terms of the future…what is *most* important to you?"

2. Make a list of four or five values by getting the *most* important and continuing with the questions, "And what else?" or, "If there were anything else what would it be?"

3. In the event of a negative answer such as "I don't know", ask the person to "just suppose" or, "Imagine you knew, what would you say?". Stick with it until you get answers.

4. Then prioritise the values by repeating them back to

the person and ascertaining the order of importance, or "motivational sequence".

5. Then feed back the values in sequence and look for compliance.

6. Finally, build the proposal for acceptance of the coaching process around the client's personal value system, to gain a greater degree of acceptance and co-operation.

CONTRA-INDICATIONS TO COACHING

It is important to note that there may be contra-indications to coaching or indications when not to get involved with coaching.

Such issues might be:

• addictive or dependency issues

• marital issues

• financial issues

• family or personal issues.

Coaches are not trained as therapists and, therefore, it is best to remember that if such issues arise or become apparent while engaging in coaching, then the "*if in doubt, refer it out*" rule applies. Suggest to the client that they may wish to take time to discuss some issues with a qualified person; that as a coach we are not qualified to assist in these areas; and that we can defer completion of the process until they have discussed the issues with others. We should remember that coaching is not meant to be counselling or therapy: such professions deal with things that have occurred in the past and may be affecting current behaviours. Coaches can come in after such interventions and take the client from where they are now to where they want to be in the future. We do not give advice; we make suggestions and bring a unique partnership to help improve the thinking and application process.

At this point it is also worth mentioning the ethical obligation of a coach to both the "client", which is usually a company funding the service, and the "coachee", who is the person benefiting from the process. On occasion, it happens that, as a result of the coaching process, the coachee realises they have no desire to remain with a company. This is a sensitive situation. On the one hand we have an obligation to the coachee to do everything we can to help them evolve successfully; on the other hand we have a duty to the client to assist them to maximise their potential. So what should we do? We are bound to confidentiality by our code of ethics, so we cannot just discuss this with the company. Currently our advice to coaches is based on the following points:

1. The coachee has often resolved to leave by the time they raise the issue. Therefore, they are already beginning a process of mental disengagement.

2. Their performance may not have been all it could have been in the first place as they may have already harboured an unconscious desire for change anyway.

3. The objectives of the company may be bettered by having a new, more committed, person within the role.

Therefore, I currently believe that it is ethical to assist the coachee to move positions, on the understanding that the needs of the company are met by the coachee positively contributing to a planned succession and handover process. This includes the coachee advising their employer of their intention to leave at the earliest possible opportunity. This way we have a means by which we can meet the needs of the client company and the coachee as ethically as possible. Experience has taught us that this is the best method to date. That and advising the client company that such situations do occur and that this is our policy when faced with this situation. We would then work with them to decide what policy is best for them, taking into consideration all the ethical and performance requirements.

CHAPTER EIGHT

The Greatest Coaching Challenges

So what do professional coaches working in the corporate field find to be the most common challenges? There are approximately seven challenges that arise most frequently and in different forms when working with business people.

1. Excellence Through Partnership

Many of our clients are already successful businesspeople. They have accomplished much in their field and yet still feel unfulfilled. They feel that there is a part of themselves that has yet to be released and sent out into the world. They are aware of their full potential but they have reached a point where they can go no further on their own.

Their sense of perspective of themselves is no longer sufficient to help them identify their additional strengths and abilities. They need an outside view from someone committed to their development who has no involvement with them and so can inform them of, and help them identify, ways to move from where they see themselves as "stuck". Often they have reached a point where they almost need "permission" to access their other resources or strike out into areas they have previously left untravelled: for example, areas of new challenge or new creativity, or areas that might further their personal and professional evolution but which are often radically different from what they have become known and recognised for.

This also applies to using the coach as a confidential

sounding board for new ideas within their business organisations. The coach often becomes a facilitator of their future thinking and helps them by providing feedback and structure on ideas that they may be considering for the future.

2. Time Management

Time is increasingly a precious commodity. In the US it is estimated that the amount of time devoted to work has increased by four weeks a year, time that has been taken from our sleep periods. Despite this extra time, people still complain of a lack of time or of the inability to manage what time they have. However, as Dr Denis Waitley puts it, "We cannot manage time, we cannot make an hour longer than it is or take yesterday back into to-day, so time management is not about 'managing' time it is about successfully managing our focus."

Coaching is about managing our focus, ensuring that at any one time we are using our time as effectively as possible. Coaching encourages us to use each precious moment to carry us forward towards our most fulfilling objectives and ensures that we stay focused on the enjoyment of the journey.

A useful technique that I use with CEOs and senior managers is to remind them of who their most important customer is – *themselves*. It is they who contract their time and provide their resources to the company so that the company can function effectively. If they were to withdraw their resources the company would suffer. However, often as managers we continually take resources away from ourselves and provide them to others. Yet there is a finite amount of resources that we can dedicate until such time as there is a need for payback for ourselves. Unfortunately, we are often too late in recognising this and the payback comes in the form of poor health and/or personal/family problems.

I usually suggest that senior company managers first take back control over their diary from their personal assistants or pre-define strict guidelines on the allocation of time. *We* should be deciding who we see and how often. We then set up "virtual meetings", meetings where we block time in our diaries to meet with our most important customer – ourselves. If we were to meet the most important of our clients we would make ourselves readily available to them, we would not permit any interruptions and we would give them our full attention. In a "virtual meeting" – where we are meeting ourselves, why would we do any different? We should then use this time to clear the decks of issues, reflect upon current challenges, get our reading done and so forth. This is not time out of the company; this is an investment in ourselves that contributes directly to the company, allowing us greater professional effectiveness, mastery of work time and the opportunity to develop boundaries for our personal time.

3. Assertiveness and Boundaries

Boundaries, and being able to assert one's boundaries, are important both in the business and the personal environment. Setting limits to what people can expect of you is important for personal well-being and business effectiveness. Yet because of the demands that business places upon us, we often reach beyond our boundaries and find ourselves stressed and unable to cope. Managers, because of the levels of excellence demanded from them, often feel that the burden of delivering on team performance falls on them personally. As a result, they may find themselves carrying out work that their employees should be doing in the misguided belief that if they do it, it will be done right. The manager then falls into the trap of having team members that are either happy to let them take on the burden of the extra work or dissatisfied because they may find themselves insufficiently challenged and so move on, placing further pressure on the already-burdened manager. In addition, such managers often find themselves having further work/projects passed on to them by more senior managers and finding themselves unable to say "no", as they feel it will create a poor impression.

In such situations, coaching helps in two ways: first, it shows managers a new way to empower their staff and "let go" enough to find that their staff are often more competent than they might have believed – and more willing to accept responsibility and accountability; secondly, it helps us to create work and people thresholds that allow us to "say no…for now". In other words, not to turn someone down flat but to have the courage to make them aware of our current responsibilities/demands and the fact that as soon as we have the capacity we will attend to their needs.

One of the techniques I suggest to clients who wish to define clear boundaries is "job profiling". Many positions have written job profiles that bear little relevance to current working conditions. Many positions have no job profiles at all – giving no clear definition to the manager of their responsibilities. I suggest that the manager re-write their job profile twice: as they feel it relates to their staff and then as it relates to their boss. Then I ask them to get two trusted staff members and have them write the manager's job profile in terms of what resources they feel the manager should be providing them with to get their work done effectively. This helps the manager get a useful picture of what is expected of them from their staff. They then compare this with their perception of what they must deliver to staff. If they have a good enough relationship with their own boss they can ask them to write a job specification, identifying what *their* manager feels are the most important things they expect them to deliver on. Armed with this information, the manager can then write a personal job profile, incorporating all of these ingredients (with the understanding that the job of a manager today is to create an environment where his team members can be successful). This helps the manager identify the boundaries they can adopt in the future.

For senior management, I find that assertiveness and boundary issues often relate to their peers. By incorporating such educational issues as the latest communications skills, planning and so on, the challenge can be about positioning and managing the politics that occur at the highest levels and how the client can best profile themselves to either retain what they already have or further advance their existing position. Such work is highly confidential and often the coach plays a valuable role in helping the client assert themselves at important times and deal with the "ego-political" issues that can arise at senior levels.

4. Clarity

Clarity of thought is an essential tool today. It concerns how we focus and the meaning we attach to the objectives we define. Clarity of thought impacts on the quality and effectiveness of our business decisions. The fast pace of corporate life today seldom allows us time for adequate reflection. Many of us work reactively rather than pro-actively, driven by the decisions and actions of others. Without reflection, there is little clarity. Information comes at such a pace and quantity that we often need to be reminded to concentrate on that which we do best.

Time with an executive coach is almost enforced reflection, a time out of time, when the services of such a trained facilitator can enable us to make leaps of insight into our challenges and future dreams.

5. Communication Skills

We are starting to experience the "high-touch" revolution. For some years now and for many to come the "high-tech" revolution has been providing us with platforms and tools to enhance our thinking, our ability to organise and communicate conveniently and cheaply over vast distances. The Internet has opened up the world and driven us onto an information superhighway on which we endeavour not to become road kill. It has challenged political systems, redefined relationships into cyber communities and banished nationally-based censorship laws.

But there has been a downside: people hiding behind voicemails, screening their calls and their interaction with others; automated sales systems that remove the human interaction from the sales process. For a time, in this technology fever, we had started to forget about the human factor. But now it is re-asserting itself and allying itself to the technology revolution to enhance its impact. This "high-touch" revolution focuses on the human aspects of business and the inherent potential within the person that helps create the teams working in this modern world. The rise of better educated, more motivated and mobile people allied to technological change has meant an even greater need for the human factor, as the world had been in danger of isolating itself into communities of one.

New professions are evolving in this 21st century

revolution: E-learners, where learning is facilitated by people over the Net; the rise of human resource departments in organisations; the increased demand for even more professional salespeople where the value of the sale is high and the human touch essential; the executive coach and trainer. All of the above are new professions of the 21st century and all require excellent communication skills. Old management had no need to interact – they simply instructed. Modern managers, however, have a high need for exceptional communication skills. They lead through facilitation, listening, learning, questioning, harmonising and all the human skills to get the best out of their people. Coaches play a large part in improving the skills of managers and applying them to the real human challenges they face every day in the process of re-creating themselves to face the "high-touch" era that is here now.

6. Working *ON* not *IN* the Team

As I have already mentioned one of the biggest challenges modern managers face is working "*in*" the team – getting all the little things done that need doing. However, they are tasked to work "*on*" the team – getting all the strategic things done that take the team into the future and deliver on their targets. This requires discipline, and often an external viewpoint to benchmark the manager's success in this regard. Coaching delivers here by keeping managers focused on the big picture and creating an environment where employees willingly take on the responsibility of their positions.

7. Life/Work Balance

In keeping with the "high-touch" revolution is a growing

sense of the importance of balance in professional careers. We often ask career-motivated clients, "Why?" "Why do you do this?" "Why is this important to you?" "What will this do for you?" to be greeted by the answer, "For my family, or kids or future".

In the past century, business used to be plagued by "absenteeism" where employees repeatedly failed to show for work. In the current era, the opposite is true: "presenteeism" rules where uncertainty prevails. In this age of constant change a "macho" culture of first in and last out has become the norm. The work takes priority: my success is based on the number of hours I am seen to put in. So we have office car parks full at 6am and the same cars still there at 10pm. But for what purpose? To impress the boss? To impress one's peers? Or to be as productive and effective as possible? Here's a secret: effectiveness is not a function of hours employed; it is a function of value invested. In coaching we work with both the client's "legs" – their business leg and their personal leg. If either leg is weak, the whole body falls and effectiveness is lost.

Burn out of top executives is no longer an option, nor is it wise. The decisions they make while under unnecessary pressure may impact negatively on the company. The decision they make to leave such a culture and join a more person-friendly environment could rob an organisation of its greatest competitive edge – the knowledge of its people. High management turnover because of poor management environment is not something that ensures business success. The company that still uses the phrase "firings will continue until morale improves" is already a dinosaur in this "high-tech/high-touch" age.

Working with internal and external coaching agents is an investment that guarantees the retention of such top management. Keeping them focused on their personal as well as their professional goals is a key tenet of modern coaching. It is the means by which we create high levels of personal commitment and personal responsibility for a company's future in an employee – when we can show them that the company shows high levels of commitment and responsibility for *their* personal futures.

CHAPTER NINE

Coaching Case Studies

To get a feel for the variety of work that is often undertaken in the coaching situation, I have included some coaching case studies. The names and the companies have been changed (or omitted) to ensure confidentiality. In each case, more than just the issues commented on was dealt with through the coaching process but I have chosen certain points by way of illustration.

CASE 1: MARK. GENERAL MANAGER HR. INSURANCE SERVICES

Mark is general manager of HR for a large financial services company. He is highly experienced, well recognised in his profession and in his mid-forties. When he came to coaching he had been tasked with the job of closing down a significant number of retail outlets, handling the personnel and union backlash from this and doing so with a skeleton HR team, which also had to run all the remaining company HR functions. He is usually a highly focused and competent individual but the stress of the task was beginning to wear him down.

In coaching he found an environment where he had enforced reflection periods in an otherwise hectic schedule. He had a non-judgemental facilitator who helped develop some new solutions to the challenges he faced. He also had an opportunity to try out some new ideas before implementation and the discipline to keep focused on the task at hand.

His views after his programme were that not only had
he improved on his usual performance by "30 per cent",
but also that he probably could not have come through
that period without the assistance of his coach.

CASE 2: GINA. NATIONAL MANAGING DIRECTOR. MULTINATIONAL MEDIA COMPANY

Gina is a young MD with an excellent track record. Each
career move she has made has been an improvement on
the last. Enthusiastic and dedicated to her work, she was
experiencing a crisis of confidence in her position after
the introduction of a matrix management structure to the
organisation had blurred reporting lines. Faced with a
degree of internal political gamesmanship and developing
power struggles, she was questioning her effectiveness and
her position within the firm. Her personal motivation was
being effected by the change and her future expectations
regarding the success of the company were being seriously
undermined.

Through coaching, we identified that she did indeed
wish to remain with the company rather than seek
opportunity elsewhere and that, in the current situation,
her work was seriously at odds with her values. Having
recognised this, she was able to re-motivate herself to the
task at hand, cut the number of direct reports on her
management team, change job roles and remove those who
were challenging her and thereby causing dissension. Her
confidence rose, her natural assertiveness returned,
company morale soared and the haemorrhaging of
personnel to competitors stopped.

CASE 3: TOM. BOARD DIRECTOR. CALL CENTRE OPERATION

Tom is a member of the board of an important call centre operation. He is a very direct person with a clear focus on the task at hand. However, his challenge concerned how he was perceived as a communicator among his peers, direct reports and team members. He wanted to develop greater influencing skills and to be more aware of the people issues that arose from time to time.

In coaching, we psychometrically profiled him and identified his critical performance gaps. Then we began a process of education and role-play during the coaching sessions, where he began to identify the communications styles of the key influencers in his field. From there we developed a "role" which he would use to interact with people. The concept of a role for him was useful as, once he was aware of the roles we all play, he was able to develop a role that would trigger his awareness of the need to be more people focused. In time, he found his influencing skills improved significantly and the need for the "role" was dropped, as he internalised his effective new communication style.

CASE 4: NIALL. OWNER/MANAGER SME. MANUFACTURING COMPANY

Niall is in his late forties and the owner of a successful manufacturing firm. His "hands on" approach ensured he worked long hours and that he was called on for every small decision. He wanted to develop the business further but was limited in terms of his time. He needed to implement computerised design systems and retain critical staff within the firm.

When coached, he started to identify the critical blocks in his behaviour that were holding the development of the business back. With the assistance of his coach he gradually loosened his hold on the reins. He promoted people and empowered them through creating "small step" development programmes. He prioritised his business and client base, identifying the most successful and then axing those that were not contributing sufficiently. With the freeing up of resources, he was better able to service important clients. Through promotion and "co-operative autonomy" he increased his retention of quality staff and initiated suggestions from the floor, thus improving the work environment and the quality of production output. He also installed and developed his computerised design system. All of this was accomplished while still managing the operational requirements of the business. What was added was the difference that better focus and the discipline of being held accountable to himself made for delivering on his plans.

CASE 5: FRANK. REGIONAL MANAGER. BANKING

Frank is a career banker. He loves the work he does and is very conscientious about the importance of his work to the firm. He manages a regional team and is responsible for delivering on their performance. However, in order to do this, he worked fifteen hours a day, five days a week. He suffered from "presenteeism" rather than absenteeism. For him it was important to be seen as first in and last out every day.

Initially he saw no problem with this until asked, "Why do you do what you do?". His immediate answer was, "For my family." When questioned further, however, the paradox between spending more time in the office "for the family" and actually not having enough time with his family (a very common work/life balance challenge) became quite obvious. His long hours were habitual; he felt that unless he put in the hours he wasn't performing effectively. So we began an experiment. For three weeks he would do two eight-hour days each week, the rest of the week he could work his usual hours. On analysing performance at the end of the period he discovered that on the eight-hour days he was by far more productive than the fifteen-hour days. The shortened deadlines put fresh impetus into his work and, therefore, increased his performance.

Over time, he extended the eight-hour period to a daily deadline. He became more pro-active about projects, improved his delegation skills, took further trainings and began spending the extra time with his family. He has since been promoted. Where he was previously viewed as being indispensable to the team's success – he is now seen as an effective people and project manager.

CASE 6: PAUL. SALES MANAGER. TELECOMMUNICATIONS

Paul, early thirties, was a very successful sales manager in the telecommunications sector. Respected by his team and his peers, he felt that he was not maximising his potential. Ultimately, he decided to leave the organisation he was with because he wished to pursue self-employment.

We had him advise his employer, choose a possible successor from within his team and create a handover process that would guarantee a seamless transfer, thus limiting the potential loss to the company. We then assisted him to exit the organisation and worked with him on developing a new venture, supporting him from the early challenges to where he had created a successful venture within the course of twelve months.

CASE 7: LAURA. SALES MANAGER. FINANCIAL SERVICES

Laura had been a sales manager with the company for some time and was concerned about the fact that she might be passed over for promotion.

While being coached she developed new ideas for her sales team that ensured that they met (and exceeded) target two quarters in a row. She developed new ideas for sales promotion with the client base, including "hot topic" short seminars, which maximised her and her team's exposure to the client base. Laura started contributing articles to industry publications and created her own team newsletter, which profiled her as the "editor" to her client base and to senior management internally.

At present, she is being considered as a possible head of sales for a new division of the company.

These are just some of the situations where coaching has made an impact.

Coaching is about effecting measurable change. In all these cases the intervention and assistance of a coach allowed people to give themselves permission to release latent potential within them. Ultimately, it is the client who creates the change, but it is the coach who creates the possibility and the process by which it is accomplished.

CHAPTER TEN

Eight Steps to Coaching as a Career

STEP 1: OBTAIN SUITABLE PROFESSIONAL TRAINING

This is easier said than done and it may be necessary to just strike out on your own at first. Coaching is an experiential and evolving profession for the 21st century. Five years ago few people were engaged in this area of business but five years from now things may be very different. At present, there are no industry-standard training institutes for training and certifying executive coaches, although there are a number of organisations that do offer a form of training, such as the Coach University based in the USA, which offers training over the internet and the telephone. Our own First Coach International specialises in training executive coaches and helps them launch their own practices or work effectively within corporations. Unfortunately, many others are opportunistic training companies and individuals offering their own brand of training, which may range from the excellent to the poor.

It is my wish that, in years to come, coaching will be the norm for business people and that both professional and training institutes with agreed standards will be founded as communities and training grounds for those dedicated to the actualisation of people's abilities. But for now here are a few pointers for the person considering coaching and looking for a suitable training provider. They should have:

- a keen and personal interest in the development of human potential. They must have a personal commitment to helping people improve and reach levels of achievement that they themselves would not accomplish alone

- experience in the field in which they are intending to coach people. This should be a proven track record in sales, management, training or human resources

- excellent communication skills and the ability to empathise quickly and effectively with clients

- clear personal and professional goals for the future and would view the accomplishment of the goals through helping their clients accomplish theirs.

As for a training provider, they should show a proven track record of coaching in the area of the market in which they wish to work (this includes the programme trainers). They should:

- demonstrate that the principles of coaching are at work within their own organisation

- be committed to professional standards and have a mission statement or code of ethics that outlines their philosophy to their clients (of which you will be one)

- demonstrate proven competency in the field and should include one-to-one coaching sessions as an essential part of their training programme. These coaching sessions should at least be over several weeks in duration – two meetings after a training does not constitute a coaching programme

- be able to show a successful training history and have past clients who are willing to speak on their behalf

- teach a systemised process of coaching that is easily replicable and is effective

- have suitable professional insurance
- indicate their future support to the emerging profession.

If these criteria can be met then it is likely that you can benefit from this provider.

STEP 2: GET A PERSONAL COACH

Should you decide to strike out on your own, then at the very least find a personal coach whose style you are comfortable with and who you can model successfully. Find one that can serve as a role model and make it clear that you wish to be assisted to be a coach yourself.

This coach should exhibit the skills you wish to emulate:

- excellent questioning and listening skills
- creative thinking assistance
- self-discipline
- a systematic coaching process
- an ability to facilitate personal planning
- an ability to gently but firmly help you to hold yourself personally accountable for your actions and success.

Also choose a coach who has the ability to remain external by keeping you to a coaching process over a period of time that helps you accomplish your goal without creating a dependency in you for their assistance.

The hardest thing to find when you are a coach is another coach whom you trust and are willing to take guidance from. When you find one hold onto them until it is time for both of you to move on.

STEP 3: EMBARK ON CONTINUOUS LEARNING

When you commence coaching, you should embark on a programme of continuous learning. Your ability to be the best of coaches will also be determined by the knowledge and the skills that you can bring to each new client. Therefore, it is essential that you embark upon a process of learning on as wide a subject range as possible. Professional business skills such as sales, management, communication, technology, career development and all the skills that are pertinent to your coaching area should be supported by a thorough background of personal development skills.

As coaches are required to help navigate their clients through an era of constant change, they require a knowledge of how and where to access the relevant information at the time it will do the client most good. Read constantly, take seminars and courses, create coaching forums with other coaches and discuss case studies. The first step to being a powerful coach is to gain knowledge. The second step is to apply it for the good of your client.

STEP 4: DEFINE YOUR NICHE

However, hard you work there will always be a finite number of clients that you can manage at any one time. You will also have a turnover of clients who feel that at a certain time they can no longer benefit from having you as a coach. This is natural and healthy – coaches should never attempt to create dependency in a client. To maximise your potential and your earnings you should, therefore, find your market niche. This will be very much dependent on your experience, learning, skill-set and personal interest. The per-hour value of these clients will also play a part in defining your niche. Is your niche sales and, if so, in what industry? It is not unusual for coaches to specialise in a particular industry and a particular field of expertise and charge for their value accordingly. It makes it easier to present a business case to a company, as you can show a proven track record in this field and how, through your coaching, a 10 per cent increase in sales revenues can more than adequately compensate them for your professional fees.

STEP 5: ESTABLISH EFFECTIVE QUESTIONING HABITS

Habits are repetitive responses – reflexes. A coach's reflex is to ask questions, in an encouraging manner, with the full expectation of a positive response. Did you know that there are (at least) six classes of question that can be used in coaching to address different scenarios? Make a study of questions and practise listening. In this busy world people often just need the time to talk and the guidance to give themselves permission to make extraordinary changes for themselves and their companies.

STEP 6: BE CONFIDENT TO BE INQUISITIVE AND DARE TO CHALLENGE

Coaches walk the talk. Our job is to take people from their comfort zones and put them in a place of personal and professional fulfilment. In the pursuit of this goal, there should be no "no go" zones (the exceptions being medical, financial or marital advice, or areas in which we may not be qualified to give counsel).

We should have an abiding expectation of and conviction in our client to make just the change they need and we should be as probing as necessary to help them see that future too. They may kick back – even clients who engage us willingly may fight us when it comes to accepting change. So be prepared to challenge them – hold them to their goals. That is our job, to help navigate clients to shores they may never have reached alone.

STEP 7: COMMIT TO PROFESSIONAL ETHICS

In a profession that is just beginning to expand, a personal commitment to acting in accordance with a code of professional ethics, one which espouses a duty of care towards clients, is an essential step. As with many emerging professions, there are no guidelines on how clients may choose a suitable business or personal coach. Anyone can set up a coaching practice – just by hanging out a sign. Fortunately, business coaching is one of those areas where results matter and where such results can be measured and quantified. This itself should eventually weed out those coaches who fail to give their all to their clients.

To establish credibility, it is useful to indicate to clients that we bind ourselves to a written code of professional ethics (perhaps similar to the one I have outlined in Chapter 5) and provide them with a copy of such a code, by which they can measure our performance for them.

STEP 8: BEGIN. START NOW

Coaching is a pro-active process. It demands the highest degree of pro-activity from the coach. If executive or personal coaching is for you, begin now. Coaches are those who help shape the world that others wake up to every morning. It is a growing and an important profession for the new century. In time, it will fulfil its most important purpose – a purpose greater than employee satisfaction, or better productivity, or more effective management, or better work/life balance, or learning organisations, or meaning in work. It will show people the way to their most important quest in life: to become everything they are capable of becoming. To change the world for good or ill, we first begin with a single will. The first will to begin with is our own.

CHAPTER ELEVEN

The Future

What is the future for this emerging profession? Where will the profession be twenty years from now? Here are some trends and predictions for the future of executive and personal coaching.

EXECUTIVE COACHING BECOMES A CHARTERED PROFESSION

It is very likely that, as the benefits of coaching make their presence felt in the marketplace, executive coaching may become a chartered profession. The demand for coaches in all fields of business, especially coaches working in external practices who contract their time to executives, will rise.

Like accounting and legal services, the provision of coaching services to businesses may become a standard. This would involve the establishment of recognised standards, professional national and international institutes, qualification through recognised training programmes for prospective coaches and the growth of accredited trainers of coaching. Executive coaching will become a postgraduate programme or a programme of further education, once a prospective coach has developed several years of experience. It is unlikely that it will be taught strictly under the current models of classroom education as executive coaching is highly dependent on human interaction skills and having reference to a wide skills-base for its success. Already a UK university is offering a

Masters degree programme in coaching and mentoring, expanding the concept to include social and community issues as well as business.

What is certain is that there is a growing and proven body of knowledge that will contribute to the success and professionalism of the next generation of coaching.

THE WIRELESS COMMUNICATIONS REVOLUTION

The growth of wireless communications and the access to the internet, video streaming, live telecasts, email and the developing personal communications revolution – available through hand-held PDAs (or Personal Digital Assistants/Palm Computers), will mean that the provision of executive coaching need not be limited by national boundaries. It is conceivable that successful coaches will attract clients worldwide who will pay electronically on a telecast, pay-per-session basis. They will even form coaching communities who "log-on" to interact about their plans and successes.

In the future, it is believed that half as many companies will do twice as much business and will earn three times the current revenues. As a result, the demand for coaches will increase to handle the needs of these executives. Companies may employ coaching practices to operate throughout their organisations on an international basis. It may not be unusual for practices to be highly specialised within certain industry segments or fields of experience, such as sales or finance, or even specific multinationals. The development of instant translators will also reduce the current limitations of language. The demand for encryption in communication software will increase, as the need to ensure the confidentiality of such e-coaching will become even more important.

Cultural coaching may become a service to help an even more connected world observe the nuances of other cultures. Profile will become important as a means of attracting the best clients and highest rates. Familiarity with technology and an ability to harness it with a "high-touch" aspect will play an important part in the future of coaching. Coaches may very well become a new breed of e-warrior, competing for business and providing the very best standards of personal service through Cyberspace.

RAPID GROWTH OF PERSONAL (LIFE) COACHING

Coaching will not be limited to business; it will also grow significantly within the personal marketplace. The skills of a coach transfer very effectively into helping others with everyday life. None of us are born with a manual for life, so many of us, with the help of a life coach, will be writing our own manuals for life, health and prosperity.

As a greater recognition grows of the importance of personal responsibility in effecting the change we want, we may see a shift from therapy and counselling sessions to a more pro-active method of handling personal issues through life coaching. We will not need to have personal problems to consult a life coach, we may just want to make some changes for our future. Working with a life coach will help us focus more on where we can be instead of focusing on where we have been. It will bring a greater degree of personal empowerment to clients, reduce the impact of "labelling" people with "complexes and conditions" and create a healthier approach towards living and society.

COACH SUPPORT SERVICES

Someone will need to "coach the coaches". It is unlikely that coaches will allow others within their practice or their competitive environment to coach them. As a result, coach support services may arise. Being a coach for the coaches will be a demanding job but a necessary one, as it will make the service currently available to coaching clients accessible to the coaches themselves, allowing them to stay on top of their game.

Wherever and however executive and personal coaching evolves in the future, it is here now and it is here to stay. The company we work for may already be experiencing its effects. If not, it will and it must soon. Our world and our workplace are changing and we all need to become people who watch over others.

Bibliography

Berens, Linda, *Dynamics of Personality Types: Understanding and Applying Jung's Cognitive Processes* (Telos Publications) 2000

Gerber, Michael, *The E-Myth Seminar* (Nightingale-Conant Corporation, audio) 1999

Lewis, Byron, *Magic of NLP Demystified: A Pragmatic Guide to Communication and Change* (Metamorphous Press) 1990

Maslow, Abraham, *Toward a Psychology of Being*, 3rd edition (John Wiley & Sons) 1998

NLP Comprehensive, *NLP: The New Technology of Achievement* (Simon & Schuster) 1993

O'Connor, Joseph & Ian MacDermot, *Introduction to NLP: Psychological Skills for Understanding & Influencing People* (Thorsons Publishing) 1998

Waitley, Dr Denis, *Seeds of Greatness: The 10 Best Kept Secrets of Total Success* (Pocket Books) 1995

Waitley, Dr Denis, *The New Dynamics of Winning: How to Use Sports Psychology for Winning in Life* (Simon & Schuster, audio) 1995

Waitley, Dr Denis, *The Psychology of Winning: Qualities*

for a Total Winner (Simon & Schuster, audio) 1995

Waitley, Dr Denis, *Winner's Edge: The Critical Attitude of Success* (Berkley Publishing Group) 1994

Index